Stop OVERTHINKING

THE COMPLETE GUIDE TO FINALLY BE FREE OF THE CLUTTERS OF YOUR MIND AND TAKE CONTROL OF YOUR LIFE

Michelle Curtery

© Copyright 2020 by Michelle Curtery- All rights reserved.

The following Book is reproduced below with the goal of providing information that is as accurate and reliable as possible. Regardless, purchasing this Book can be seen as consent to the fact that both the publisher and the author of this book are in no way experts on the topics discussed within and that any recommendations or suggestions that are made herein are for entertainment purposes only. Professionals should be consulted as needed prior to undertaking any of the action endorsed herein.

This declaration is deemed fair and valid by both the American Bar Association and the Committee of Publishers Association and is legally binding throughout the United States.

Furthermore, the transmission, duplication, or reproduction of any of the following work including specific information will be considered an illegal act irrespective of if it is done electronically or in print. This extends to creating a secondary or tertiary copy of the work or a recorded copy and is only allowed with the express written consent from the Publisher. All additional right reserved.

The information in the following pages is broadly considered a truthful and accurate account of facts and as such, any inattention, use, or misuse of the information in question by the reader will render any resulting actions solely under their purview. There are no scenarios in which the publisher or the original author of this work can be in any fashion deemed liable for any hardship or damages that may befall them after undertaking information described herein.

Additionally, the information in the following pages is intended only for informational purposes and should thus be thought of as universal. As befitting its nature, it is presented without assurance regarding its prolonged validity or interim quality. Trademarks that are mentioned are done without written consent and can in no way be considered an endorsement from the trademark holder.

Table of Contents

Headaches	13
Chronic Pain	13
Frequent Sickness	14
Insomnia and Decreased Energy	15
Decreased Libido	15
Digestive Issues	16
Appetite Changes	17
Depression	17
Rapid Heartbeat	18
What Is Self-Talk?	25
Importance of Positive Self-Talk	25
How Positive Self-Talk Works	27
Tips for Practicing Positive Self-Talk	28
Learn to Be Okay With Your Flaws	33
Embrace Your Flaws Whether They Be Physical, Mental, or Emotional	34
Understand the Importance of Being Confident	34
Record It	37
Figure Out How to Meditate	37
Keep a Journal	38
Relinquish the Past	38
Stop Multi-Tasking	38
Organize	39
Put Routine Decisions on Auto-Pilot	39
The Amount of Information You Receive Should Be Limited	39
Why Are Breathing Exercises Needed?	43
What Types of Breathing Exercises Exist and How Do They Work?	44
Breathing Techniques	44
Breathing Exercises for Relaxation and Anxiety	47
Taming Tactic #1: Positive Affirmations	53
Taming Tactic #2: Listening to Yourself	56
Taming Tactic #3: Avoid Procrastination	59
Taming Tactic #4: Get a Hobby	61
Taming Tactic #5: Be Lovingly Patient With Yourself	63

Top Causes for Overthinking	67
Areas in Life That Cause People to Overthink	70
Create a Safe Haven	75
De-Clutter and Organize Your Living Space	76
Yoga, Tai Chi, and Physical Mindfulness Practice	77
Grounding	78
Dietary Changes	78
Affirmations and Manifestation Exercises	79
Journaling	80
Start Thinking Three Times More Efficiently!	83
Further Work: From Theory to Practice	85
Introspection: What Do You Remember First?	85
Develop the Freedom to Act on Instinct	91
Don't Make External Rewards Your Source of Motivation	92
Never Be Satisfied but Be Grateful	92
Live Life on Your Terms	93
Don't Let Off the Pressure	93
Don't Compete With Others	94
Always Seek to Learn New Things	95
Own Your Mistakes	95
Worries and Anxiety	99
Fight or Flight	99
Structured Problem-Solving	100
Limit Your Consumption of Media	100
Try Meditation or Aromatherapy	101
Take a Shower or Hot Bath	101
Exercise	102
Rest and Experience Freedom Like no Other	102
Case Study	104
Principles of a Minimalist Approach	107
Your Home, Your Digital Life, and Your Activities	110
Panic Attack Medical Cures	116
Panic Attack Self Help Cures	116
Finding the Source of a Panic Attack	117
Positive Self-Esteem	119

Protective Self-Esteem 119
Low Self-Esteem 119
Learn How to Alter Your Life With Self-Esteem 120
The Construction of Teen Self-Esteem Starts at Birth 123
Conclusion 127

Introduction

What exactly is overthinking?

The Ancient Greek stoic thinker, Socrates was perhaps onto something when he proclaimed: "The unexamined life is not worth living."
However, I would add that the overly examined life isn't one I would personally recommend either.

And then there's Descartes' mantra "I think therefore I am," that didn't catch on as much as it did for nothing!

Thinking is though I don't mean to claim this ground-breaking idea as my own pretty darn useful. And by calling out overthinking, I do not by any means wish to discourage deep thinking in itself. Rather, as with any addictive and self-destructive behavior, overthinking is harmful. It takes what are perhaps the most valuable abilities we possess as a species critical thinking and imagination and turns them up to 100, burning out our minds and our emotional capacity along with it.

In fact, if you tend to overthink, it can be completely ravaging to both your mental and physical processes. It sends the brain's stress response into overdrive, inducing the fight-or-flight response. As a consequence, your brain and body are flooded with the stress hormones cortisol and adrenaline and not only during those sporadic and brief periods where danger is imminent, as this response is designed for, but any time your thoughts start to wander into overthinking territory...

In this sense, you could say that Humanity actually evolved to become a species of overthinkers. Despite our cognitive ability putting us literally a head and shoulders above the Animal Kingdom, we still have the same primitive fight or flight mechanism, but now whipped up into a toxic cocktail with our human love of thinking. Essentially, we are now doomed to "think ourselves into stress." Thanks to our ruminating brains no threat is ever truly gone! The things you lie awake thinking about at night are any of them an immediate threat to your life? Does thinking about them incessantly ever solve anything?

Since our nervous systems haven't been able to keep up with our newfound thinking abilities they continue to flood our bodies with the hormones to keep us alert and panicked enough to spring out of harm's way and so we stay perpetually alert... and perpetually ready to run. Is it any wonder we can't switch off? Or that anxiety, insomnia, and panic disorders are becoming increasingly widespread in the modern world? We end up physically and emotionally exhausted, oscillating between jittery anxiety and overwhelming, apathetic fatigue, once our body's overused adrenaline supply eventually dries up.

Overthinking Explained: Is Overthinking a Disorder? Why Is It Bad?

So, to start right at the beginning. What is overthinking? Why does it happen? And what's the difference between rumination, introspection, problem-solving, and self-reflection? I must first clarify that in most cases, although not ideal, overthinking is not necessarily pathological or cause for medication, and you can work on overcoming it all you need is the right techniques and advice. However, it does require a thorough understanding of the thought mechanisms, the neurophysiological response, and the triggers so that you are aware of what overthinking looks like, why you do it, and most importantly how to stop it in its tracks!

As mentioned, overthinking isn't a disorder or an illness in itself. Rather, it's a trap we all fall into from time to time. And although this means no one is exempt, on a more positive note, it also means no one is cursed with it forever!

However, overthinking is still a potentially harmful and self-sabotaging habit that should be taken very seriously, as when an individual can't stop obsessing and irrationally worrying over things in the long term, and regardless of circumstances (in other words, it's not a temporary state due to a particular life event or a temporary concern), it can interfere severely with their mental health and quality of life.

All in all, overthinking is as common as breathing in this modern world of both endless possibility and endless stress. The worries of the world are just one click or swipe away, and our sphere of concern is stretched far beyond its natural limitations biologically intended only for a select few in your family or tribe. In today's reality of globalization and digital connectivity, we are exposed both to more information and more trauma and this doesn't go unnoticed by our subconscious. It's a prodigious thing to be able to communicate and receive news from all four corners of the world, but our poor minds are not wired to expand our empathy to such a degree. Therefore, we are not mentally prepared to process so much emotional stimulation and cope with such a fast-paced world. Is it any wonder, then, that our minds tend to spiral out of control if we don't make the required effort to keep ourselves grounded?

Many clients also have complaints of reliving past failures, mistakes, or traumas over and over again; they feel simply unable to move past them, forgive themselves or heal and move on. Many also struggle to stop their relentless worrying about their goals and future tasks until they feel almost impossible to accomplish. And for others, it's the obsession with what others think of them that keeps them up at night. Did I offend them? did I embarrass myself? What must they think of me? And so on.

"I'm Just Problem-Solving." The Difference Between Overthinking and Problem-Solving

You may be one of those overthinkers that claim it's all just necessary problem-solving. "I can't pretend my problems don't exist" or "someone has to think about these things" may be mantras of yours when having to explain your deep thoughts—either to others or just to yourself. However, it's an easy mistake to make to confuse overthinking with innocent problem-solving. You might convince yourself that letting your worries spin around your mind in this way is productive. However, don't forget that the solution to a problem doesn't tend to come more easily simply by thinking harder. In fact, some of our greatest emotional clarity comes from adequate physical and emotional rest and distancing one's worries.

Think of it this way: a simple definition of problem-solving is actively looking for the solution to an issue. You will know if you are problem-solving when you notice a decrease in stress as you work on untangling the mess of thoughts you were presented with. On the other hand, overthinking involves over-analysis and rumination (which I will come to next!). This only spurs you to dwell on your worries and prevents you from having the mental capacity to coin a solution for yourself. Overthinking magnifies every minute issue, or even unlikely possibilities making you focus on the worst-case scenarios as though they are already set in stone.

Indeed, the human mind is cruel like that; the more you think, the more darkness you create for yourself causing you to be stuck in a state of perpetual anxiety.

Chapter 1: Effects of Overthinking

Undoubtedly, overthinking causes many effects on people's lives. This can be in the form of developing an anxiety/depression order, lowering one's self-esteem, or even causing one to be unable to work towards their goals. Overthinking is actually a huge stressor on the person that is impacted. This causes a lot of undesirable symptoms to arise in a person's life. Stress is one of the main effects that arise from overthinking and can cause a variety of emotional and physical symptoms. Let's take a look at how overthinking and stress can impact a person's life.

Headaches

Just like acne, many scientific studies have found a relationship between high levels of stress and headaches. This includes pain that is in the head or neck region. One scientific study that tested this relationship consisted of around 250 people that were suffering from chronic headaches. The scientists found that within those people, 45% of them had recently endured a stressful event. A similar but larger study found that the increased number of headaches that occurred over one month was associated with an increase in stress intensity. If that's not enough evidence, another similar study focused on 150 military professionals at a clinic specialized for headaches. They found that nearly 70% of those who had headaches said that they are stress-induced. This makes stress the second most common trigger for headaches. Lastly, other common triggers of headaches can include dehydration, alcohol consumption, and lack of sleep.

Chronic Pain

People commonly report that they have an increased number of pains and aches in their bodies when they are under a lot of stress. One study that focused on this relationship consisted of about 40 people that had sickle cell disease. They found that when they had increased levels of stress daily that they also felt an increase in pain as well. Another study focused on studying cortisol, the stress hormone, and how it is also associated with chronic pain when its levels are increased. For instance, there was a study that consisted of 16 people who reported having chronic back pain. When they studied them further, they found that these people had high levels of cortisol. Another similar study found that people who reported having chronic pain had higher levels of cortisol within their hair. This is an indicator of someone who has been under prolonged stress. Again, bear in mind that these studies have shown relationships between stress and chronic pain, but we still have to consider other factors that could be playing a role as well. Moreover, it is still unsure whether chronic pain causes stress or if stress causes chronic pain. This is something that still needs to be further studied. Several other factors could be playing a role in increasing chronic pain, such as; nerve damage, poor posture, injuries, and age.

Frequent Sickness

If you are someone that feels like you are always sick, or always battling allergies or a case of sniffles, stress can be the culprit. Stress takes a huge toll on people's immune systems, which will put them at a higher risk of infections. In a recent study, a group of 60 adults was given the flu vaccine. They found that the people who had a weakened response to that vaccine indicated that stress is related to decreased immunity. In a similar study, over 200 adults were selected and split into two groups; low stress and high stress. Throughout 6 months, 70% of the people that were in the high-stress group experienced respiratory infections. They also had 60% more symptoms of the illness compared to the low-stress group. In addition to this study, another similar study showed that a person's increased susceptibility to developing a respiratory illness was linked to increased levels of stress. Again, more of these relationships still require further research as the connection between stress and immunity is a complex one. Although stress is related to a person's immune health, it can also be caused by other factors such as multiple myeloma, leukemia, physical inactivity, and a poor diet.

Insomnia and Decreased Energy

When a person is under high levels of prolonged stress, they can begin to feel that they have decreased levels of energy and chronic fatigue. For instance, a study of over 2000 participants reported that tiredness and constant fatigue was in fact, associated with high-stress levels. Stress also affects a person's sleep cycle and could cause conditions like insomnia, which could be the cause of fatigue. A small study found that people who had high levels of stress related to work were associated with restlessness before bed and increased sleepiness throughout the day. Another study that also consisted of over 2000 participants found that people who experienced higher numbers of stressful events were associated with an increased risk of insomnia. Similar to other symptoms, these studies show a relationship but they may not be accounting for other factors that may be causing the symptom. More research in this area is required in order to directly define the relationship between stress and fatigue. Other factors that can cause fatigue include; underactive thyroid, a poor diet, low blood sugar, and dehydration.

Decreased Libido

Numerous people experience a change in their sex drive when they are going through a stressful time. A small study that focused on a group of 30 women evaluated their stress levels and then had them watch an erotic film to measure their arousal. The women that had higher levels of stress reported less arousal compared to those that were less stressed. A similar study that was larger consisted of about 100 women that found that high levels of stress were directly associated with their lower levels of sexual satisfaction and activity. In addition, a similar study focused on over 300 participants and found that the people who reported that they had high levels of stress found that their sexual satisfaction, arousal, and desire were negatively impacted. Again, you must also consider other factors that may be contributing to a person's changing libido. This could include psychological causes, fatigue, and hormonal changes.

Digestive Issues

When people are experiencing higher levels of stress, they tend to have problems with their digestive system, such as constipation and diarrhea. In one study, they had nearly 3000 children that participated, and they found that when they were exposed to stressful events that they had an increased risk of constipation. Stress also affects people who already have digestive disorders such as inflammatory bowel disease (IBD) or irritable bowel syndrome (IBS). These two disorders share traits such as constipation, diarrhea, bloating, and stomach pain. In another study of almost 200 women, they found that high daily levels of stress were linked to an increase in their digestive distress. In addition, an overall analysis that focused on 18 different studies that explored the relationship between stress and digestive diseases, found that almost 75% of these studies have found a relationship between a person's digestive system and stress levels. We have to keep in mind that although these studies show a strong association, more studies are required to look at how stress impacts a person's digestive system. Other factors can also cause digestive issues such as; medications, infections, physical activity levels, dehydration, and diet.

Appetite Changes

One of the most commonly reported symptoms of stress is a change in a person's appetite. When people are feeling stressed out, they often are showcasing two extremes; they're either raiding their fridge in the middle of the night, or they have no appetite or desire to eat at all. A scientific study that focused on students in college found that around 80% found that they had appetite changes when they were under high stress. Out of this population of students, nearly 40% experienced a decrease in appetite, while around 60% reported an increase in appetite. In a similar study of around 100 people, they found that these people, when under stress, exhibited behaviors like eating even when they are not hungry. A person's change in appetite can also be caused by weight fluctuations during high-stress times. For instance, a study of over 1000 people found that weight gain in overweight adults was associated with stress. Although these studies show a strong association between the change in a person's appetite and stress levels and weight, more studies are required in order to further understand what other factors could be involved. Other factors include; psychological conditions, hormonal shifts, drugs, or certain medications. ù

Depression

Certain studies suggest that the development of depression is related to chronic stress. One study that consisted of around 800 women that had depression found that the beginning stages of their depression were heavily associated with them having chronic or acute stress. Another study discovered that higher levels of depressive symptoms were associated with increased levels of stress. This study consisted of around 200 adolescents. In another study, a study of around 40 people that had major depression found that their depressive episodes were related to stressful life events. Keep in mind that these studies have shown associations between depression and stress, but it does not mean that every case of depression is caused by it. A lot more research is required on this topic in order to 100% confirm the role that stress plays as it relates to depression. Other factors that aren't stress that contribute to depression include certain medications, environmental factors, hormone levels, and family history.

Rapid Heartbeat

Symptoms of high-stress levels often include an increased heart rate or a fast heartbeat. One study that found an association between stress and rapid heartbeats discovered that a person's heart rate is much higher when they are going through a stressful situation. Another similar study focused on about 100 teenagers, and they discovered that an increase in heart rate was caused by undergoing a stressful task. In addition, another similar study exposed about 90 students to stressful tasks and found that they had increased blood pressure and heart rates. Interestingly, however, they found that playing relaxing and soothing music during that task prevented a rapid heartbeat. An increased heartbeat can also be caused by other factors such as drinking alcohol, caffeine, heart conditions, thyroid disease, and high blood pressure.

Chapter 2: ADD; AD/HD AND SOCIETY

It seems that many people in the health care professions do not accept the idea of adult ADD; AD/HD or acknowledge what the condition means for adults. People who experience the condition need to be understood and listened to. They often find it challenging to conform to societal expectations, with negative consequences to their self esteem
research also draws attention to the need for teachers to be better prepared to reconise and respond to ADD; AD/HD in the school system. The people who took part in the study spoke about the difficulty of going through school without having a name for the issue that was affecting them.

All of the people who took part in the research study spoke about the importance of support from family members and friends
ADD; AD/HD can bring many challenges to family life. Like any mental health problem, everyone is affected when someone in the family has ADD; AD/HD. It will be by investing in family supports that we can ensure that, in the future, ADD; AD/HD will be just a feature of the person's individuality

ADD; ADHD AND ANXIETY
If you have ADHD, it may be difficult to recognize the symptoms of anxiety. ADHD is an ongoing condition that often starts in childhood and can continue into adulthood. It can affect your ability to concentrate, and may result in behavioral problems, such as:
- hyperactivity
- lack of attention
- lack of impulse control
- fidgeting and trouble sitting still
- difficulty organizing and completing tasks

An anxiety disorder is more than just feeling occasionally anxious. It's a mental illness that is serious and long lasting. It can make you feel distressed, uneasy, and excessively frightened in benign, or regular, situations.
BUT How can you tell the difference?

If you have anxiety, you may be unable to concentrate in situations that cause you to feel anxious. On the other hand, if you have ADHD, you'll find it difficult to concentrate most of the time, in any type of situation.
If you have both ADHD and anxiety, the symptoms of both conditions may seem more extreme
Though a professional evaluation is necessary, family members may be able to tell the difference between ADHD and anxiety. The key is to watch how your symptoms present over time.

HOW TO RESOLVE THE OVERTHINKING FOR ADD; ADHD PERSON

The ADHD brain worries too much about "what ifs" and "could be." You need strategies to calm your anxiety, reset your compass, and get back to sleep at night

ENGAGE IN HEALTY DISTRATION

Distracting yourself is the fastest way for many people to stop ruminating. The trick is finding the distraction that works for you. Manual hobbies keep the mind distracted
External distractions can be annoying and distract you from what you need to stay focused on, but you can always take steps to minimize them by closing your door or wearing a noise-reducing headset. It is the internal distractions that are the most challenging for the ADHD brain.

BE LIKE A JOURNALIS: To put the brakes on this nagging worry don't allow anyone to get into your head and after the breathing exercises write your emotions on your diary

PRACTICING MINDFULNESS
Sometimes we don't need an external factor to start worrying. All we need to do is overthink things that haven't happened yet. Life's uncertainties can be a great distraction. Practicing meditation and doing breathing exercises is helpful in calming those "what ifs" that consume our thoughts.

GET MEDICAL HELP
The habit of worrying is often due to insecurities about liking or doing something wrong. Everyday stressors, perfectionism and unpredictable situations cause it, but the cause can be much deeper and involve past trauma, codependency or neuroticism. Seek help to get to the root of the problem.

ACTION, HOWEVER SMALL Action,
Much of our fretting can be diminished by taking action. If you're worried about your health, make an appointment with your doctor to get a checkup and discuss your concerns. Ask for advice on ways to develop healthier habits.

TALK THINGS WITH A FRIEND
Talking a problem over with a friend quiets racing thoughts. She might have helpful advice to put your worries in perspective. Even if your concern is an annoyance that can't be fixed, sharing your worry will help you feel better. A problem shared is a problem cut in half.

CHANGE YOUR PROSPECTIVE
Some of our worries stem from unrealistic expectations of ourselves, so we need to adjust our goals or reframe our negative thoughts in a more positive way. If it's other people that bother you, remember that you can't expect perfection in an imperfect world.

Chapter 3: How to Stop Overthinking — With Positive Self-Talk Technique

What Is Self-Talk?

Self-talk is the inner discussion that you have with yourself. Everybody engages in self-talk. However, the impact of self-talk is only evident when you are using it positively. The power of self-talk can lead to an overall boost in your self-esteem and confidence. Moreover, if you convince your inner-self that you are beyond certain emotions, then you will also find it easy to overcome emotions that seem to weigh you down. If you can master the art of positive self-talk, you will be more confident about yourself and this can transform your life in amazing ways.

You can't be sure that you will always talk to yourself positively. Therefore, it is important to understand that self-talk can go in both directions. At times, you will find yourself reflecting on negative things. In other cases, you will think about the good things that you have achieved. Bearing this in mind, you must practice positive self-talk. This can be understood as pushing yourself to think positively even when you are going through challenges.

If your self-talk is always inclined to think negatively, it doesn't mean that there is nothing you can do about it. With regular practice, you can shift your negative thinking into positive thinking. In time, this will transform you into a more optimistic person that is full of life.

Importance of Positive Self-Talk

Research shows that positive self-talk can have a positive impact on your general well-being. The following are other benefits that you can get by regularly practicing positive self-talk.

Boosts Your Confidence
Do you often feel shy when talking to other people? Maybe you don't completely believe in your skills and abilities. Well, positive self-talk can transform the perceptions that you have about yourself and your abilities. Negative self-talk can hold you back from achieving things in life. It can even prevent you from even trying in the first place. Unfortunately, this can drive you to overthink the things that you feel as though you should do. So, instead of acting, you end up wasting your time overthinking about them.

Positive self-talk lets you put aside any doubts that you could have about accomplishing a particular goal. Therefore, you will be motivated to act without worrying whether you will succeed or not. You're simply optimistic about life. There is nothing that can stop you from trying your best when attending to any activity.

Saves You From Depression
Overthinking can make you more susceptible to depression because you garner the perception that you are incapable of performing well. Frankly, this affects your emotional and physical well-being. Some of the effects that you will experience when you're depressed are lack of sleep, lethargy, loss of appetite, nervousness, etc. Positive self-talk can change all of this. It will fill you with the optimism that you need to see past your challenges. As a result, instead of believing that you can't do it, you will begin to convince yourself that you can do it. Positive self-talk can transform how you feel, it's just a matter of changing how you perceive the world around you.

Eliminates Stress

There are many stressors that we have to overcome every day. The truth is that we all go through stress. The only difference is how we deal with stress. Some people allow stress to overwhelm them. Often, you will find such folks with a negative outlook on life. They will have all sorts of negative comments about life. "Life is hard," "I can't take it anymore," "I'm always tired," "Things never get easier," etc. We've heard such comments coming from our friends who have given up on life. The reality is that stress can get the best of you if you surrender. Practicing positive self-talk can help you realize that stress comes and goes. It is a common thing that everybody experiences.

Protects Your Heart

We all know that stress is not good for our health. Stress leads to many diseases including cardiovascular diseases such as stroke. Therefore, by practicing positive self-talk, you will be protecting your heart.

Boost Your Performance

Positive self-talk can also help boost your performance in anything that you do. There are times when you find yourself feeling tired and dejected. For instance, when you wake up in the morning feeling as though you ran several kilometers, this can be draining. It affects how you attend to your daily activities. With positive self-talk, you can tap into your energy reserves and boost your performance. It is surprising how you can quickly change how you feel by thinking positively.

How Positive Self-Talk Works

Before getting into detail about practicing self-talk, it is important to understand how negative thinking works. There are several ways in which you can think negatively, including:

Personalizing
This form of negative thinking occurs when you blame yourself for anything bad that happens to you.

Catastrophizing
If you expect the worst to happen to you, then you are simply catastrophizing everything. The issue here is that you don't allow logic to help you understand that some things are not the way you think.

Magnifying
Here, you pay more attention to negative things. In most cases, you will block your mind from thinking positively about any situation that you might be going through.

Polarizing
You look to extremes when it comes to judging the things that are happening around you. From the perceptions that you have developed in your mind, something is either good or bad.

Tips for Practicing Positive Self-Talk

Have a Purpose
There is a good reason why you will hear most people argue that it is important to live a purposeful life. Undeniably, when you strongly believe that you are here on this earth for a good reason, you will strive to be the best version of yourself. You will be constantly motivated to try to achieve your goals in life. The best part is that you will feel good about your accomplishments. This is because they are an indication that you are heading in the right direction towards your goals. Therefore, when practicing self-talk, always look to a

higher purpose that you yearn to achieve. This will keep you on the move without worrying too much about the number of times you stumble.

Get Rid of Toxic People

It is common to have a bad day. We cannot deny the fact that there are times when life seems difficult. Usually, this happens when our emotions overwhelm us. Despite this fact, some people have these bad days every day. They never seem to stop talking about their worst experiences. Unfortunately, this can take a negative toll on your life, especially when interacting with other people. Picture a scenario where you are always told about how life is difficult. Your friend keeps mentioning to you that life has changed and you can't realize your dreams. In time, this is the mindset that you will also develop. There is nothing good that you will see in your life since you can't think positively. The interesting thing is that you might actually be making positive changes, but you will unlikely notice.

Never Compare Yourself to Others

It is easy to compare yourself to other people more so when you feel that you lack something. Sadly, such comparisons only push you to look down on yourself. The comparison game will blind you from seeing the valuable qualities that you have. You will develop a negative attitude towards your abilities as you assume that other people are better than you. By expressing how you are thankful for what you have, you can identify the numerous things that make you different from other people. This is a great way of developing your personality and helping you believe in yourself.

Talk Positively With Other People

Talking positively with other people will have an impact on your self-talk. If you constantly talk about negative things with those around you, then there is a likelihood that you will also engage in negative self-talk. There are probably numerous times where you've heard people say that you become what and how you think. Therefore, if you keep focusing on the negative, expect negativity to flow through your mind. Stop this by trying your best to surround yourself with positivity, starting with the way you talk to other people.

Believe in Your Success
The best way of propelling yourself to succeed in your endeavors is by believing that you can do it. If you don't believe that you can do it, then this holds you back from trying anything. This should be applied to everything you do. For example, if you are working towards losing weight, you should convince yourself that you can do it. This is the first step that will give you the energy you need to overcome challenges on your way to success.

Overcome the Fear of Failure
Succeeding in life also demands that you should overcome the fear of failure. You should always bear in mind that your failures are learning lessons. In fact, most people who have succeeded in life have failed at some point. When you overcome the fear of failure, you will be more than willing to try anything without hesitation. This opens doors to plenty of opportunities. The good news is that you will have learned a lot from the experience of failing.

Use Positive Affirmations
You can also give a positive boost to your self-talk by using positive affirmations. The best way to use these affirmations is by writing them down. Note them somewhere you can easily view them. For instance, you can stick them on your refrigerator or your vision board, if you have one. The importance of positioning them in a convenient place is to

guarantee that you motivate yourself every day. Ideally, this is an effective strategy of training your mind to always think positively. Examples of positive affirmations that you can note down include:
- "I am blessed."
- "I am a successful person."
- "I embrace what life offers me."
- "I am happy today."
- "I allow myself to be filled with joy."

Avoid Dwelling in the Past

When you think too much about the past, it will likely be difficult to focus on the present. This will have an impact on your self-talk. If you keep regretting the mistakes that you have made, there is a good chance that you will think negatively. Your emotions will blind you from thinking clearly. As such, this can have an impact on the decisions you make.

You must find a balance between thinking about the future and the present. When thinking about your future, focus on the positive. If there is something that you want, think in that direction and convince yourself that you already have it.

Chapter 4: The Importance of Self-Imagine

Self-love is the biggest factor that contributes to believing in yourself and letting go of negative feelings. No love is more important than self-love. If you cannot love and respect who you are then no one will love or respect you either. It's like the kid who always makes fun of himself in class. Just because he is laughing doesn't mean he thinks it's funny. It means he is insecure, and he wants to point out the flaws he believes he has before anyone else can do it because it hurts less if you hear it from yourself. You cannot mask your true feelings and if you don't work through them, it will eat away at you. That kid is making fun of himself because he doesn't love everything about himself.

If you love yourself flaws and all, you aren't going to want to cover it up when you are being hurt. You are going to defend yourself and defend everything about you because that's what makes you who you are. If you are 100% happy with yourself, you won't have to worry about negative thoughts running through your mind all day. You will be able to push them to the side and feel confident you are being the best version of yourself.

Learn to Be Okay With Your Flaws

Knowing and understanding that everyone has flaws and being okay with your personal flaws can make a huge difference in the way you think about and handle situations in your life. Sorry to say, but you are not perfect. Guess what? That's okay. No one is. Everyone has their own set of fears, flaws, and self-doubt. The trick is to expect them and accept them. Some of these flaws can be worked on, and in time maybe you can change them. Like cooking, or typing with more than one finger. However, there are others that you just can't and that's okay too. You may take longer writing a paper or struggle to understand math. So, that's why we have auto-correct and calculators. The best part about technology is we do not have to be perfect.

Embrace Your Flaws Whether They Be Physical, Mental, or Emotional

Have you ever been referred to as clingy in a relationship? As long as it's not crazy clingy, I promise you will find someone who loves your clinginess. Wanting to be with someone who makes you feel good all the time isn't a flaw, it's human nature. Finding the right person who enjoys spending as much time with you as you do with them will happen; don't give up and don't stop being who you are.

Are you self-conscious of the scar on your face because people have stared and laughed, or simply because you see it as an imperfection? Learn to love it, appreciate it, respect the way it got there, and accept the fact you cannot change it nor should you want to. Let me tell you, my husband has a scar above his left eye from an accident he was in as a child and I think it is one of his most attractive features. It gives him character; it tells a story.

Understand the Importance of Being Confident

If you are confident in who you are, you won't feel the need to second guess yourself or overthink your choices.

The importance of being confident is not to be arrogant. We don't want you to feel like you are perfect and it's your way or no way. Being confident means, you are okay with yourself just the way you are, flaws and all.

Confidence shows. Wear it with pride. Walk into your meeting knowing you are going to nail it even before it starts.

STOP OVERTHINKING

Walk into an interview knowing you have the job before you even meet the interviewer; walk into your gym knowing you are going to crush that 3-mile run before you even start the treadmill. When you go into any situation with confidence, you have much more of a chance of accomplishing your goals. Why? Because you are dedicated, you want it, you want to prove to yourself and to others that you have what it takes. Being confident is being strong; it's believing in yourself and cheering yourself on in every situation you come across.

Chapter 5: How to Declutter Your Mind and Be True to Yourself

The vast majority of us have a mind brimming with clutter. There is something more terrible than having a cluttered home or workspace, and that is having a cluttered personality. A cluttered personality is anxious and unfocused. It attempts to move in a wide range of bearings immediately and the outcome is quite negative.

Mental clutter can incorporate the majority of the following: agonizing over the future; ruminating about the past, keeping a psychological plan for the day, and grumblings. Luckily, there are methodologies and strategies you can use to wipe out some space in your mind.
Beneath you will discover the different ways to de-clutter your mind so you can quit feeling so overwhelmed, accomplish more, and get greater clearness.

Record It
You do not have to keep everything put away in your mind. Pick an apparatus—it very well may be an online instrument, an application, or even a stack of paper—and consider it a capacity gadget for each one of those odds and ends of information that you have to recall. This can incorporate arrangements, telephone numbers, and thoughts for future ventures.

Figure Out How to Meditate
Fundamentally, contemplation is figuring out how to concentrate the brain totally on the present minute. When you figure out how to put the majority of your consideration on a certain something, for example, your breath– every single other idea vanishes. It is nearly what could be compared to

taking your brain through a vehicle wash and having futile and pointless musings washed away.

Keep a Journal

Keeping a diary is like the last point, record it yet with more profundity. A diary enables you to download the inward prattle that is always interfering with your point of view when you are attempting to complete significant things. For instance, you can write in your diary about the accompanying things that you are stressed over; plans for accomplishing a significant objective, or even worry about a relationship that is depleting your vitality.

Relinquish the Past

Mind clutter is regularly identified with the past. A great many people keep an enormous bureau of mental drawers put away in the back of their minds. These drawers are loaded up with slip-ups they have made, open doors they have missed, individuals they have harmed, and past complaints. Set aside the effort to experience those psychological drawers and dispose of recollections of the past that are not serving you well and are simply cluttering up your present life.

Stop Multi-Tasking

On the off chance that your home is a wreck and you have to arrange and de-clutter it, how might you start? You would most likely begin by picking one significant territory—for instance, the kitchen table—and clearing it of all clutter.

What could be compared to tidying up the kitchen table is to pick a specific measure of time which you will commit solely to one significant undertaking. During that time push all psychological clutter to the side and spotlight the majority of your consideration on the job needing to be done.

Picture a table that is clear everything being equal, except the one undertaking which you will take a shot at. Ensure that the table avoids every single other thing during the whole piece of time that you have committed to this assignment. On the off chance that whatever else attempts to work its direction onto the table, drive it off.

Organize

Nothing makes as much mind clutter as an unending daily agenda. Acknowledge that you cannot do everything, and center on the things which are most essential to you. Make a short rundown of your top needs, and ensure that the main part of your mind space is committed to the things on that rundown.

Put Routine Decisions on Auto-Pilot

Little, routine undertakings can involve a great deal of cerebrum space. This can incorporate things, for example, the accompanying:
- Choosing what you are going to wear every day
- Choosing what to have for breakfast every day you wake up
- Settling on a choice on what to have for your main meal

You can diminish the measure of brain space that is taken up by these normal errands by putting them on auto-pilot.

The Amount of Information You Receive Should Be Limited

An excessive amount of information can stop up the cerebrum. This incorporates the information that you take in every day by perusing papers, online journals, and magazines; staring at the television screen; taking an interest in internet-based life; surfing the web on your advanced mobile phone, etc.

Limit the measure of information that comes into your life—and make space in your cerebrum by doing the accompanying:
Set a limit on the measure of time that you will spend via web-based networking media locales or perusing the web. Withdraw from any online journals and drop any magazine memberships that are not adding to your personal satisfaction or your prosperity. Ensure that the sentiments that you focus on originate from well-respected people with pertinent qualifications. Choose the information that is significant to you and neglect everything else.

Chapter 6: How to Control Overthinking in Few Minutes

Respiratory gymnastics is one of the most effective ways to put our physical and physiological states in order. Breathing unites the body and mind. Breathing exercises can help us relax, control feelings of anxiety, relieve stress, overcome insomnia. They are even useful for improving attention and help drive away negative thoughts.

We will look at various breathing techniques, find out how and why they work, as well as the pros and cons of each of them. How to do breathing exercises?

What is the use of breathing exercises? Why do you need to do it? Discover breathing exercises that can help improve your health and tone your body.

Why Are Breathing Exercises Needed?

Breathing is vital—the body supply with fresh oxygen and exhaled carbon dioxide from the body. But not only that, but your breath also changes depending on your mood. If you are stressed, you breathe quickly and shallowly. If you come to rest, the breath slows down again. But those who often breathe shallowly strain the body. Breathing deeply and correctly is therefore useful against stress and promotes health and well-being. If you consciously concentrate on your breath, you also breathe deeper and into your stomach.

You can calm the body and relax with various breathing exercises. You don't need much time for the following activities, and you can always integrate them into everyday life—in case of stress, in the office, before falling asleep, or before exciting situations.

What Types of Breathing Exercises Exist and How Do They Work?

The use of various breathing techniques and methods of controlling breathing to calm the soul and body is not new. There are breathing exercises for health and tranquility, breathing exercises anti-stress, breathing techniques for the lungs and bronchitis, breathing exercises for children, and even breathing exercises for weight loss and the abdomen. In the East and Buddhist culture, this has been practiced for centuries. The activities of conscious meditation also base on breathing control techniques. How to breathe?

The practice of deep breathing stimulates the parasympathetic nervous system, which is responsible for the involuntary activity of the body when we are at rest. The method of shallow or shallow breathing enables the sympathetic system, which is responsible for the activation of various organs. The sympathetic nervous system is activated when we are under stress and causes what is commonly known as a reaction: "fight or flight" ("hit or run"). Our task is to learn to "remove" such conditions using various breathing techniques.
Of all the automatic human reactions, breathing (like blinking) is one of the few that we can consciously control. It is a kind of portal to the autonomous system of our body through which we can transmit messages to our brains. Next, we will consider various types of breathing techniques and exercises that can be used both in general and in certain specific situations.

Breathing Techniques

Clavicular Breathing
This type of breathing is also called the upper chest. Since

this type of breathing is of the thoracic type and is superficial, the bin does not allow the lungs to expand as it does with deep breathing. How to find out if you are using this type of breathing correctly? Place one hand on your chest and the other on your stomach, and breathe normally. Which of your hands rises higher? Some people raise both hands. If so, then the breath is deep enough and correct.

Clavicular breathing is ineffective since the most potent circulation that provides our body with oxygen occurs in areas below the lungs. Accordingly, if a person uses only clavicular breathing, not enough oxygen enters these areas. Since it is quick and shallow breathing, the blood enriches with less oxygen, which leads to a lack of nutrients in the tissues.

Diaphragmatic or Abdominal Breathing
This type of breathing is also known as abdominal or deep breathing. What is the diaphragmatic breathing technique? With such breathing, muscles of the diaphragm activate, and air also enters not only the upper but also the lower part of the lungs. In this case, you see how your stomach rises, hence the name. To many, abdominal breathing seems strange and unnatural. Perhaps because a flat stomach is now in fashion, and therefore many people, especially women, restrain their abdominal muscles, thus preventing deep breathing.

Since childhood, we used to hear from mothers and grandmothers—"pull your stomach in." Besides, constant tension and stress can be the cause of muscle contraction of the abdominal cavity (the so-called nerve tic in the abdomen).

Advantages of diaphragmatic or abdominal breathing: this breathing technique altogether provides our body with oxygen, allowing it to function fully. In this case, the heart rate decreases, as does blood pressure.

Cons of diaphragmatic or abdominal breathing: this type of breathing has no drawbacks, except one—you need to learn this technique because not everyone knows it automatically.

Thoracic or Bone Breathing
Also known as chest or rib breathing. With bone breathing, intercostal muscles are involved, with the help of which the chest expands. This type of breathing is usually not used by itself; it is part of full or mixed breathing.

Full Breath
Full breathing also has many names in various sources—abdominal, mixed, bone-abdominal, costal-diaphragmatic, lower costal. With full breathing ("inhale fully"), a stream of air enters through the nostrils, passes through the nasopharynx, trachea, and bronchi, and fills the lungs, which increase in volume. With deep breathing, the abdomen rises, the chest, the diaphragm zone are activated (located between the chest and the waist).
Pros of complete breathing: this breathing technique helps the body calm down and relax. The body receives a large amount of oxygen, lowers heart rate, blood pressure, and decreases the level of cortisol in the blood—the "stress hormone."

Cons of full breathing: while the technique of abdominal or deep breathing can buy to automatism, in the case of concentrated breathing, this does not happen, this technique is not easy to apply, mainly if you have never used it. The method of full breathing is the basis of breathing exercises, which we will now consider.

t

Breathing Exercises for Relaxation and Anxiety

Why are you worried about anxiety? Maybe this is a symptom of depression? Find out with the cognitive neuropsychological test for depression right now! Before you go in for breathing exercises, find a comfortable place.

Full Breathing Technique for Relaxation

One of the most effective techniques for reducing anxiety is full breathing. For the correct performance of this gymnastics, we must know what types of breathing are. How to exercise?

Place one hand on your chest and the other on your stomach. Breathe so that only the arm that rests on the chest rises. Hold the air and then exhale it through your mouth. Repeat several times.

Now, on the contrary, breathe so that only the hand lying on your stomach rises. The chest should not move. Repeat several times.
Now try to take turns breathing so that first the arm lying on the stomach rises, and then the arm lying on the chest.

After you master the preceding technique, breathe deeply, using both types of living at the same time. In this case, make small pauses between inhalation and exhalation. Inhalation and exhalation should last equally.

Asymmetric Breathing Technique

Another useful technique for relieving anxiety and relaxation is a short breath and a long breath. For example, try breathing so that the exhalation lasts 5-6 times longer than the breath. It is a beneficial exercise because the heart rate increases on inspiration and decreases in exhalation. Thus, by delaying expiration, we enhance these effects.

Resistance Breathing or Artificial Respiration for Relaxation

The resistance breathing technique is to create resistance on expiration. It can do in various ways: for example, exhaling air through closed lips, teeth, through a tube, or even by singing. We can exhale the sound of the mantra "Ohm" or by merely vibrating our vocal cords. This sound resonates with the chest and head, creating a delightful feeling.

Dynamic Breathing for Relaxation

There are relaxing breathing techniques that require a little imagination. As you inhale, imagine a pleasant wave covering you from head to toe. Feel every part of your body, and if there is tension somewhere, try to remove it. As you exhale, imagine that the wave is retreating. How to understand that you are relaxed? We can say that relaxation was successful if you feel a slight tingling or warmth at your fingertips.

Make Breathing Exercises a Good Habit

To master respiratory gymnastics and make sure that it helps, you need to exercise regularly. How to set up a training regimen?

Find yourself in a cozy and calm place where you can comfortably sit or lie down.

Do not be discouraged if you cannot immediately complete the exercise correctly. Gradually learn, no one immediately succeeds entirely.

Try to do it every day for no more than 5–10 minutes. If you want, you can increase this time—no need to set ambitious goals right away.

Exercise at the same time, for example, before bedtime or

immediately after waking up. So, you can quickly turn breathing exercises into a habit.

To learn the necessary breathing exercises for asthma and COPD, direct instructions are helpful and essential. During a training course, you will learn how to breathe correctly in addition to many other necessary things. However, some more straightforward exercises can also try out yourself. The breathing exercises presented here primarily intend to make your chest flexible and deepen your breathing.

Breathing Exercises While Lying Down

Abdominal breathing: An essential technique and the basis for many other breathing exercises is the practice of abdominal breathing or diaphragmatic breathing, which significantly reduces the work of breathing. Lie on your back in a relaxed position and place both hands on your stomach. Now try to breathe in such a way that you can notice the lifting and lowering of the abdomen. Breathe in through the nose and out with the lip brake.

Stretch your chest: Lie on your side and bend both legs and the upper arm slightly. The hand of the upper arm is on the back of the head. If you inhale, slowly turn your upper body backward. However, make sure that the knees are on the floor and stay tight together. As you exhale, slowly return to the starting position. Repeat this several times, then switch sides.

Breathing Exercises While Sitting

Abdominal breathing: If the abdominal breathing works well while lying down, you should practice it while sitting in the next step. To do this, place your hands on your stomach and try to breathe directly toward your hands. When you exhale, press lightly on the abdomen with your hands. It is how you support exhalation.

Stretch your chest: Sit straight on a chair without leaning. The hands hang down sideways. If you breathe in, now move one arm over the side as far as possible over your head. The upper body tilts a little to the side. As you exhale, slowly return to the starting position. Again, do several repetitions per side.

Chapter 7: Dealing Negative Thoughts With 5 Tactics

Begin by asking yourself this question: How many of your thoughts have helped you get to where you are today? How many thoughts have hindered your progress?

Your answer will tell you how in control of your thoughts you are. Overthinking makes you realize how little control you have over your mind and why there is a need to change that. A wandering, distracted mind will never give you the kind of life you long for. The kind of life you hope you. The kind of life you deserve. Our mind is overstimulated these days, and it has a lot to do with the lifestyle we lead. Take a good look at your life (and the lives of many others), and you'll see many factors that have become the reasons for your unsettled mind. With so much going on every day, your mind is not given the space it needs to observe the way it functions. For years you've probably lived with a wandering mind, unable to recognize how this negative habit is impacting your life. Until now, that is.

Taming Tactic #1: Positive Affirmations
Positive affirmations can help incredibly shape your life. For the overthinking, anxious, and wandering mind, this is exactly what you need in your life. Your ability to stay positive and maintain positive thoughts will determine the tone of your emotional life. The specific words you use to describe what is happening to you and the words you use to deliberate the way you feel about external events will trigger the kind of emotions you feel. Whether these emotions are happy or unhappy is entirely up to you.

When you choose to see things positively and constructively, when you choose to look for the good in every situation and person, you're strengthening your mind's natural tendency to gravitate toward a more cheerful disposition. People who are optimistic and positive weren't born that way. They trained themselves to be the way they are. They've gone through tough moments in life too. No one in this world is sheltered from the curveballs and ups and downs that life will toss your way. The reason why they manage to still keep a smile on their face while you struggle even trying to get your thoughts together is that they've trained their mind to gravitate toward positivity.

Your overall quality of life is determined by how you feel from one moment to the next. An overthinker's goal should now be to use positive affirmations as a training tool to keep yourself thinking about what you want out of life instead of focusing on all the things you don't want that are fueling your overthinking tendencies. You need to talk positively to yourself all the time. If you can do this with negative talk, then you're capable of turning that language around and making it positive too. It's going to require more effort, but it can be done. You need to keep repeating positive states so many times until your brain is finally convinced, and your fears disappear. This is not going to happen overnight, so you need to keep persisting until change starts to happen, no matter how long that takes.

Affirmations have the power to work because they can program a person's mind into believing a concept. It helps you visualize and believe in their goals, dreams, and abilities. In other words, you are affirming yourself and helping yourself make positive changes to your life goals. According to Heinz Kohut, the pioneer of the psychology of the self said that the fear of failure is often directly connected to a childhood fear of being abandoned either emotionally or physically. When we face failure, we tend to over-calculate the risks we are taking and work out the worst possible scenario, which is usually the emotional equivalent of our parents or guardian deserting us. We imagine an entirely dreadful scenario in our minds that we convince ourselves that trying to change isn't a good thing at all. Thus, it makes us lose out on opportunities for success, and then when we actually do fail (because our mind is already convinced, we'll fail anyway) the whole experience of affirmation that we give ourselves is that we are not cut out for success, or it is not in our karma to succeed, and then, we settle.

Your new habit is going to be to start each day on a positive note. Wake up every morning and say, "I love my life, and I love myself as I am. I love that I have a job to go to. I love that I have a way to earn a living to put a roof over my head and food in my belly. I love the challenges that the day brings because it is an opportunity for growth." There are so many positive statements we could draw on once we start focusing on them. Once positive affirmations become a habit, your life starts improving. Your productivity rises, your motivation increases, and you start getting better at paying attention to whatever it is you're doing.

To start putting positive affirmations into practice, several steps need to be done:
- Number #1: Begin by making a list of all your negative qualities. Include any criticism that others have made of you and those that you have been holding onto. Remember that we all have flaws, so avoid being too judgmental or harsh on yourself. By acknowledging your mistakes, you can then move forward and work on your flaws, and you can make a shift in your life. When you write these down, take note to see if you are holding any grudges along the way or holding on to it.

• Number #2: Now, start writing out an affirmation on the positive aspect of your self-assessment. Use powerful statement words to beef up this assessment. Instead of saying, "I am worthy" say "I am extremely cherished and remarkable."

• Number #3: Practice every day reading this affirmation loudly for 5 minutes at least three times a day in the morning, afternoon, and at night before going to sleep. You can do this while shaving or putting your make-up on, or when you are fixing yourself a cup of tea, or if you are in the shower. Look in the mirror and look yourself in the eye. Repeat these positive statements. Write these affirmations in your notebook at any time you feel like it. To enhance the impactful power of these positive affirmations, include body movements such as placing your hand on your heart when you felt uncomfortable writing out negative criticism of yourself.

• Number #4: As you work on reprogramming your mind to alter it from the concept of affirmation to a real and definite personification of the quality that you see, what would help would be to get a friend, partner, or family member to repeat for example, if they tell you that you're cherished and remarkable, and then connect with these statements by reminding yourself this is how someone you care about perceives you. If you are not comfortable with doing this with someone, then look at your reflection in the mirror and reinforce your positive message.

Taming Tactic #2: Listening to Yourself

All the criticism and the failure you've experienced up to this point have probably taken a toll on your self-esteem and confidence. It's hard not to doubt yourself when you seem to experience one setback after another. You'll be criticized and judged by others, and you'll probably criticize and judge yourself. That's the way life is, you can't please everyone. Some people will be happy with you, and some won't. Negative voices and whisperings will be all around you. They'll be in your mind, and they'll be in the voices of the people who tell you that you can't do something. It's too risky. You're not experienced enough. You'll fail. It can't be done, and you'd be foolish to try. Negativity will try to shake your belief in yourself. But when you're being drowned out by all those voices telling you "You can't" do something, remember this: No one can see the vision that you have.

Other people don't know your heart. They don't know what's on your mind. They don't know your goals, your ambitions, your hopes, your dreams. They don't know what's going on beneath the surface. For example, no one will understand how much it means to you to overcome your excessive thoughts unless they've gone through something similar themselves. So why allow your decisions to be based on their opinions? Why hold yourself back from something you want in life because other people told you that it's impossible to achieve? Their opinions and their judgments are only scrambling the thoughts in your mind, distracting you from the bigger picture. If you're going to tame your mind, you need to find the courage to trust yourself again so you can block out anything else that's trying to drown you.

Other people and even your mind will try to nudge you in all sorts of directions, which may lead you away from your goal. But the choice is always yours whether you want to listen to these voices or not. You can choose to follow what they try to dictate, or you can choose the more powerful path: Listen to yourself. Feeling like you have to stand up and do what's right alone can feel scary. But if you don't learn to trust in yourself again, you'll always be at the mercy of other people's opinions and their agenda, and that is a much scarier prospect to be faced with.

Despite all the noise and all the overwhelming thoughts in your mind, there is some part of you that always knows what the right thing to do is. Call it your inner voice or intuition. Your gut instinct has always been there, but you've forgotten to listen to it because you've been overthinking. Sometimes the right thing to do may be the hardest thing to do, and you're going to need that courage and faith in yourself if you're going to pull it off. How do we learn to trust ourselves? By aligning every decision that we make with our core values. When core values lie at the heart of every decision, every goal, and every relationship you encounter, you can trust in the fact that you're not going to choose anything that is going to result in a disastrous outcome for you. No one will know what you need or what's best for you more than you will. Therefore, the only voice you should be listening to is yourself.

Train your mind to be comfortable with uncertainty. Things are not always going to work out the way you want them to. There will be things that you will know and can know, and there are things that you may never know or come across. When it comes to overthinking, people who do this have somehow trained their brains to focus on the unknown instead of the known. They look into uncertainties and try to solve something they do not know. Some questions can be answered, but overthinkers tend to dwell on those that they cannot answer. You need to now train your brain to either seek answers from the source of the questions that you are overthinking or keep telling your brain that it is okay not to know the answer at all. Either way, trust that the decision you make is going to be with your best interest in mind if you listen to what your mind and your heart are telling you.

Taming Tactic #3: Avoid Procrastination

Sometimes the urge to put off something unpleasant can be too strong to resist. But putting it off doesn't mean your mind is going to be at peace about it or you're going to feel happy about it. In fact, you're only delaying the inevitable, and when that moment catches up to you again, you feel stressed, overwhelmed, and anxious as you scramble to do what you should have started on long ago. That's procrastination. You know you're going to have to do it eventually. You can feel the pressure building as your mind starts getting restless. Yet, you do it anyway, and you're not the only one either.

Procrastination affects everyone in one way or another. It's a lot more complex than bad time management or laziness. A few subsets of psychology have a different way of looking at procrastination. Neuropsychologists refer to this as: "A failure of executive function" or "the way you prioritize and plan ahead." Social psychologists refer to procrastination as: "A problem that relates to emotional regulation" or "An attempt to avoid negative emotions like stress." Evolutionary psychologists, on the other hand, believe that procrastination: "Could be partly due to genetics." Despite the different perspectives on procrastination, the one thing all researchers can agree on is that this is a habit that is not good for anyone.

This is a habit that has been around for a while. In 700 BC, the Greek poet Hesiod wrote about procrastination when he said: "Do not put off your work until tomorrow or even the day after tomorrow. A sluggish worker will not fill his barn, nor one who puts off his work. Industry makes work go well.

But a man who keeps putting off his work will always be at hand-grips with ruin." In a study conducted in 2014 by the researchers at the University of Colorado, Boulder, it seems that procrastination could be part of our evolutionary makeup. To figure out the genetic link, what researchers resorted to was to study pairs of twins and their work habits. Fraternal twins who only shared certain DNA were compared against identical twins who share all their DNA. Since each set of twins grew up together exposed to the same external environmental factors, their responses were compared to determine if their genetics corresponded to their procrastination habits. A mathematical model was developed by the researchers to calculate whether procrastination was inherited. What they discovered was that half the time, the difference in the twins' procrastination habits could be attributed to the differences in genetics. What the researchers also found out was that putting things off and reacting impulsively were behaviors that could be inherited together too.

Still, procrastination can't be blamed entirely on genetics. Self-regulation, the way you manage your goals, your values, beliefs, and perception play a role in your tendency to procrastinate too. Canadian psychology professor Timothy Pychyl says when you procrastinate, you're giving in to what feels good. In other words, when we're faced with negativity as overthinkers so often are, procrastination is a way to cash in on that short-term good feeling. It is an attempt to run away from and avoid bad feelings like stress, for example, if the task you're faced with is unpleasant. Pychyl and other researchers believe that the trouble comes when you tend to use excuses habitually to put off the things you need to do.

It is useful to recognize the typical words we use when we are procrastinating: "Not yet..." "I don't feel like it..." "Wait..."

"You can do it later..." with the emotions that accompany them. You need to activate an internal "radar" that recognizes when you start entertaining thoughts of procrastination. Observing your thoughts, you will learn to recognize the words you use to procrastinate. While everyone tends to put off things once in a while, doing so chronically will only lead to higher stress levels and a mind that is restless and finds it difficult to focus.

To tame your mind and avoid the temptation to give in to these negative thoughts that tempt you to procrastinate, it helps to break down the things you need to do into smaller, manageable chunks. That way, you train your mind to feel accomplished each time you complete one of these chunks and prepare to move on to the next one. Accomplishments lead to feelings of positivity, and tasks seem less intimidating when they're smaller and seemingly easier to handle. Keep your mind calm by reminding yourself there's no need to pile on the pressure to get everything done at once. It's okay to work in small steps if it helps you focus better. Find a workflow rhythm that works best for you based on your schedule, not someone else's expectations.

Taming Tactic #4: Get a Hobby

Negativity, overthinking, anxiety, and any other mental health issue you may be dealing with can rob you of your happiness. When you lose that happiness, one of the things you lose is the interest in what you used to love to do. You start to neglect the things that once put a smile on your face, the ones that ignited your passion because you're so consumed by negativity. But when you're overthinking or dealing with anxiety is precisely the time you need to fall back on your hobbies. Having a hobby gives you comfort. It gives you something to focus your mind on at a time when you need it most. It takes away the focus from the lonely, isolating feeling that often accompanies those who battle with overthinking and anxiety daily.

Hobbies are important because they remind you of your drive. They remind you that there are still things you love, even when you feel alone and miserable. When you immerse yourself in the hobby you love, the rest of the world seems to fade away. You're not thinking about what happened yesterday, last week, last month, last year, or even several years ago. You're not worried about what's going to happen tomorrow or a week from now. When you throw yourself completely into your hobby, you're actually more present than you've ever been. You forget about everything else that may be going on in your world, and for that moment, it's just you and the hobby you love.
If you don't have a hobby that you particularly love, there's no better time to start one than now. If you can't quite think of a hobby just yet or need more time to find one, a hobby you can consider to tame your anxious mind is reading. There's a quote by C.S. Lewis who said: "We read to know that we are not alone." That quote couldn't be more apt for this moment because those who deal with negativity and anxiety often do feel alone, and like the rest of the world don't understand them. That disconnect from their relationships can take a toll mentally and reading is an escape. A chance to get lost in another world, to lose yourself in someone else's inspiring stories.

The concept of reading to feel better is called Bibliotherapy, and what makes this form of therapy different is how it uses an individual's relationship or issues and connects it with the content of the books. It's interesting to know that you can overcome the challenges you may be facing by reading about how the characters in the book overcame their challenges.

It's a way for overthinkers to take their anxiety, stress, and depression and channel it or relate it to the contents of books. Reading about how the characters or inspiring individuals in those books overcame their toughest adversities is telling your mind if they can do it, why not you? If they could find the strength to keep fighting, why not you?

Overthinking, anxiety and depression can be like a ball and chain that weighs you down, stopping you from going where you want to go. Reading is a fantastic hobby for taming the mind. It's something we can all do, and reading is something a lot of people actually enjoy doing already. If you're one of those people, picking up this hobby is probably going to be one of the easiest strategies in this entire book. Remarkably, a simple hobby like reading can bring about such monumental change. This is just one example of what a hobby can do for you. Never give up on what you're passionate about because that drive will be the one that takes you out of any obstacle you will ever face in your life.

Taming Tactic #5: Be Lovingly Patient With Yourself

It's going to take time to retrain your mind. Along the way, you're bound to feel frustrated and defeated when it feels like you're not progressing fast enough. But you must do your best to be lovingly kind to yourself. Allow yourself time to absorb all the changes you're trying to carry out. Every time you successfully carry out a strategy, it's important to pause, slow down, and take a couple of minutes to celebrate what you just did. This reminds your mind that you are progressing, and change is happening. With every strategy you overcome, you're getting better one step at a time.

When you're lovingly kind to yourself, you're less impatient and more compassionate and understanding. Your perception starts to change bit by bit, and you start viewing situations and the way you react to them more objectively. You become more rational, and finally, you'll reach a point where you experience your emotion without allowing your thoughts to spiral out of control when you do. Self-compassion is what so many of us are lacking today. To survive in this high-pressure digital world, we've been forced to become adept at being self-critical when we fail to meet the unrealistic standards set by society. We've become so good at telling ourselves off for our failures that we forget to show ourselves compassion. But that self-compassion is what your overanxious mind needs right now more than ever.

To tame your overthinking mind, you need to carve out time to be self-compassionate. Since depression, negativity, and anxiety are the three enemies of a happy life, there is a need to appreciate the role of what self-love and being kind to yourself can do for you. If you can show compassion, love, and care for the people in your life that mean the most to you, then you certainly can do this for yourself too. The Loving Kindness Meditation is going to be helpful in this context. Also known as the Metta meditation, the goal of this meditation is to cultivate an attitude of kindness and love towards everything around you, even your own enemies and also to the sources of stress. This meditation involves breathing deeply to open your mind to be more loving to your loved ones and the people in this world. The key to this meditation is to repeat the message as often as possible until you feel an attitude of loving-kindness. This meditation is created to promote feelings of compassion and love for oneself and the people around them. It can help in anger, resentment, and frustration as well as interpersonal conflict. You can look forward to reducing anxiety, depression as well as PTSD.

Chapter 8: The Overthinking Core Problem

People think all the time. One does not even have to think about thinking; it just happens. That is because one never stops having words going through their minds even when he or she is sleeping.

When does thinking become too much?
Thinking becomes too much when a person thinks about a particular thing stuck in his or her head repeatedly. Most of the time, the thoughts are usually negative, thus causing demotivation, stress, anxiety, and depression in a person.

Top Causes for Overthinking

What causes people to be incapable of getting thoughts out of their heads?

Re-Living Past Experiences

Do you still think about how your sister embarrassed you in front of your fifth-grade teacher?

It is common that when a person thinks about experiences, he or she not only dwells on the negative aspects but also continuously experiences them. A person's mind may go back to the time when he or she posted a sexist comment on Twitter, or when he or she blew an opportunity, or when he or she did not pass the job interview.
A person's mind usually picks up on negative experiences from the past because the experiences went contrary to the person's expectations. However, if things went according to plan, then the thoughts become happy memories.

Mulling Over Present Experiences

Overthinking about things one can do without actually doing them is a waste of time, primarily if fear and worry motivate the person.

Has the sun not come out yet? Forgot about it. Did you just run out of cereals? Buy some. Did you forget where you left your car keys? Ride the bus. Does she love me? Ask her. Is there something wrong with me?

When a person overthinks, he or she misses out on life's precious moments. He or she does not notice the baby that smiles at him or her from across the street or the raindrops that fall on his or her windscreen.

Anxiety for the Future

Do not bite your nails too hard, or at all.

Anxiety for the future is called Anticipatory anxiety. Anticipatory anxiety is usually draining for people as it can go on for months before an event happens.

A bride may think about where her wedding will be, which service providers to contact, or who to put on the guest list. While such kind of thinking may help her to put plans into place, the thinking may cause an anxiety attack when it becomes too much.

The thoughts people allow in their minds specifically focus on what they think might happen, often with dire predictions about an event. The nature of negative forecasting about the event will be the difference between an anxiety level that is debilitating or a little uncomfortable.

Clear your headspace and live in the present.

Creating "What-If" Scenarios

"What if" situations are useful when a person is thinking

about different outcomes of certain risk factors.
However, when a person continually agonizes over issues and assumes adverse outcomes, the habit becomes detrimental overthinking about events that might not ever happen in the future stops one from going with the flow of things and from being his or her best self.

Self-Introspection
When self-introspection comes from a place of self-gratification, it can turn negative. Habitual, negative, and excessive thinking about oneself brings about depression, anger, frustration, and indifference.

When a person thinks about the bad things that happened to him or her, or about the people who do not like the person, or about all the things he or she wanted but never received, or about all the things that he or she has done wrong, that person will ultimately suffer Anxiety and depression.

Finances
Financial stress can affect nearly every area of a person's life. While it is prudent to handle financial stress head-on, it is not wise for one to dwell on thoughts of lack of enough finances.
Difficulty in paying one's bills can be stressful, but overthinking closes a person's mind to find possible solutions to the problem. Other financial situations that can cause overthinking include being in considerable debt, losing a job, having medical bills, and irresponsible spending.

Household Tasks
Household tasks may sound menial but can be significant sources of overthinking. A person may encounter stressful situations when he or she has to clean, service the car, pay the bills, cook, shop, and take care of children and pets.

However, one should not be too worried about how to get everything in order because health is more important. One can develop a work plan on how he or she will go about doing all the household chores. He or she does not have to do all the tasks in one day. That would be a more balanced and practical approach.

Loose Ends
Unfinished tasks that a person thinks about throughout his or her day can bring about life friction and stress. The small loose ends can turn into big distractions. That is because they prevent a person from being productive, or from doing his or her work.

A person can avoid overthinking by dealing with loose ends. He or she can finish the work as soon as possible, set new deadlines, or put the task on hold.

Projects
Excessive workloads with impossible deadlines can make one feel overwhelmed and under immense pressure to perform. Such situations cause people to think about overachieving continually, which may not be a healthy practice.

Concerns About People
Sometimes a person may be concerned about what other people think about him or her. He or she should accept that they cannot control other people's thoughts. However, a person may recognize that stress is contagious, and other people's concerns should not drag him or her down.

Areas in Life That Cause People to Overthink
People spend a lot of time thinking through life to accomplish great things. Thoughts lead to inventions and discoveries. However, thinking about both great and small achievements in life can lead to overthinking.

Here are some of the areas in life that cause people to overthink:

Work

It is natural for one to want his or her boss to think highly of their work. That can be a good thing when it motivates a person to work better. However, such an aspiration loses meaning when a person always worries about being in their boss's good graces.

Similarly, when a person seeks perfection in all the tasks that they do, he or she may end up second-guessing themselves. As a result, the person overthinks and stresses about how to do things correctly.

Additionally, an individual may fall into the trap of comparing themselves to other workmates. One needs to understand that there will always exist differences between any two people in the workplace. Some people may be more experienced because they have advanced in their careers while others are just starting. Avoid making comparisons and stick to your lane.

Relationships

Overthinking is the cause of many broken relationships. It may also be the reason why a person has difficulty in building strong relationships.

When a person overthinks, their mind continually thinks about things and consequently arrives at different conclusions. That causes the person to keep changing their mind, a factor that causes indecision in relationships.

In addition, people who overthink have encyclopedic memories of things that a person said to them. Therefore, one can easily pick up on a comment other people said to him or her, 6 months ago, during a fight. Re-opening wounds that are meant to heal does more harm than good to any relationship.

Besides, a person who overthinks will need constant reassurance from their partner, and such behavior may be emotionally draining for the partner. Eventually, if the partner does not understand, the relationship could end due to trust issues.

School
Schools provide a suitable environment for people to think academically and get excellent scores in their exams.
It is easy for one to become stressed and anxious under the pressure of making significant academic gains. Stress and Anxiety are the results of overthinking. Every person in school knows the importance of doing tests, and they do not want to fail.

When preparing for an examination, classrooms become crucibles where students exhaust their thoughts to the end. When students overthink, they tend to underperform because their minds are not in a state that facilitates learning.

In some countries, society places extreme importance on school. As a result, the schools put students under immense pressure to perform and to produce good results for the school to keep up with the school's reputation.
Around the world, there are cases where students commit suicide because of not being able to keep up with the demands of their school.

Health
With the increase in health risks among individuals around the world, many people worry about their health. Concern for one's health is a good practice, as it causes a person to

avoid habits that could risk their health.

However, overthinking becomes toxic when a person thinks that they will fall sick or that something terrible will happen to them. When people go through life-threatening experiences with their health, they tend to become paranoid about the possibility of the event happening again. That is understandable but not excusable.

Overthinking is not a medical concept, but the habit can have a substantial impact on health. People who keep up with negative thoughts and Anxiety may experience stomachaches, headaches, or even migraines. Overthinking has a connection to mental health issues like post-traumatic stress and borderline personality disorders.
Overthinking also causes hormonal imbalance by breaking down brain chemicals required for feelings of happiness. In addition, overthinking can cause one to have high blood pressure, a condition that causes artery damage, dementia, and strokes.

Chapter 9: How to Find Instant Zen

Meditation is an easy and logical next step for any empath. It can be very uncomfortable, at first, to sit quietly all alone with your thoughts. Try to remember that the purpose of meditation is to let those thoughts and emotions come, and then release them. Allow them to wash over you the way waves move over your feet when you walk along the seashore, crashing up and then quickly, gently, fading away.

You can also meditate on specific subjects or questions that you struggle to comprehend. The purpose of meditation is not to stir anxiety, though, so if you note repetitive, obsessive, or negative thought patterns, you may want to change your approach before your next session.

If you are already well-practiced in meditation, you might want to further challenge yourself and awaken your third eye chakra by challenging your thought patterns. Some metaphysical guides suggest using inquisition to aid this process, continually answering each of your thoughts with the question: "Is that true?" If that method feels combative or sparks feelings of internal conflict, you can instead practice disbelieving your thoughts, entertaining the possibility that the truth is the opposite of what you perceive it to be.

Create a Safe Haven
To ensure that self-care becomes a regular part of your new routine, you'll want to make space for it in your life—literally. Even if it has to be inside a closet, make sure you find some space to create a safe haven for yourself. You could also think of it as a peace bubble, meditation space, or a spiritual altar. The idea is to create an ideal space in which to center yourself whenever life outside this haven starts to

feel overwhelming. You may want to fill it with candles and crystals, smudge sticks, plants, cozy pillows, and blankets. If you relish the endless potential of a blank slate, your haven might be completely bare, dark, and quiet. There is no right or wrong way, only the way that feels right for you.

De-Clutter and Organize Your Living Space

Now that you've created a safe haven, your next goal should be to arrange the rest of your living space in a way that helps you to feel balanced, organized, efficient, and at peace. Even if you don't consider yourself a visual or materially oriented person, the way your home looks matters; it is the first thing your eyes see every morning when you wake up, and the last thing you see before you fall asleep at night. Its appearance makes a mark on your dreams and subconscious world, as well as on your conscious thought processes. Furthermore, the way it smells, sounds, and feels is important, too.

If you find the theories of feng shui resonate with you, then go ahead and evaluate the layout of your home and furniture, and rearrange whatever you have to in order to respect its principles. This is especially recommended for geomantic empaths—feng shui is also sometimes called "geomancy," and it addresses the same energetic frequencies that geomantic empaths are attuned to.

If there's no time for a full interior redecoration effort, then instead, you may want to focus on clearing unwanted energy from your living space. Take a mental inventory of the items on display in your home. How many of them were items you chose based on desire? How many did you choose based on necessity? Be on the lookout for gifts you've received, and remind yourself that you are alone and no one is judging you before you ask yourself: how do I really feel about these items that were given to me? Do they have sentimental value and represent a feeling of love and affection for me?

Or, were some of them given by people who were trying to manipulate or influence my behaviors? Do some of them remind me that people in my life don't actually get me or understand who I am?

If so, don't feel ashamed for acknowledging it. Sometimes, gifts are not given from a place of generosity, but in an attempt to exert willpower. Recognize these items in your home as centers of negative or stagnant energy, and give yourself permission to dispose of them, give them away, or send them to remote storage.

Yoga, Tai Chi, and Physical Mindfulness Practice

Exercise is undoubtedly good for the body and soul, but it can be even more effective when combined with mindfulness. Mindfulness is the concept of heightening our awareness of things we usually take for granted or have learned to ignore, like our breathing or thought patterns. Yoga is especially popular, as it addresses the need for physical alignment and mindfulness, promoting focus, relaxation, acceptance, and self-love. It can also be tailored easily to suit many different needs, sometimes fully embracing its spiritual element, or at other times being exclusively concerned with the physical body. You can easily find a yoga class to attend, and there are many schools of yoga to choose from, depending on your desire to enhance strength, find balance, repair injury, or find deeper relaxation. You can also practice alone in your home or outdoors in nature.

Tai chi also stimulates mindfulness through a series of slow, controlled physical movements. Generally, yoga can pose more of a physical challenge, whereas Tai chi requires a great deal of patience and focus, so it challenges the mind. It also looks more like a dance form, so those who feel freed by creative expression may prefer tai chi to other similar practices.

Grounding

Grounding is theoretically easy, but will only be as effective as the amount of energy you channel into the practice. All you need to do is remove your shoes and socks, plant your feet on the ground (ideally in a place where you feel a strong connection to nature), and imagine you are growing roots like a tree. Many empaths will close their eyes, breathe deeply, and utilize some form of meditation or affirmation during their grounding practice.

One mantra that you might find useful is the alternating repetition of two phrases; first, "I am one with the universe," where you may substitute the word "universe" with "all things" or the name of a higher power in your faith; and secondly, "I am distinct, unique, powerful and purposeful." These two phrases articulate polarized sentiments that many empaths mentally seesaw back and forth between; the goal here is to honor both ideas as part of the same universal truth.

Some empaths find this practice especially powerful near oceans, historical landmarks, or sites of natural phenomena, like volcanoes or earthquakes. Grounding is highly recommended for geomantic and precognitive empaths.

Dietary Changes

Every living being, whether plant, animal, or human, is made of energy. So, if you are consistently consuming foods that carry forms of negative energy, it can manifest in your body as chronic pain, illness, malnourishment, or even as an emotional symptom, like depression.

An elimination diet is a simple way to effect major change in your personal energy field, and it usually provokes rapid change. You may be very surprised to find aches or points of tension are suddenly released, although you never even noticed them before they were flushed away.

Intermittent fasting can also be a useful tool to enhance mental clarity, though it should be done with caution. Those who lead highly active lifestyles or suffer from nutritional imbalances may find this practice dangerous.

Affirmations and Manifestation Exercises

Have you ever had the experience of feeling overwhelmed by a mental to-do list, only to write it out on paper or tell someone else about it, and suddenly realize that it's easily doable, and not worth stressing over?

Or, have you ever felt that a dream or wish was too far out of reach to entertain—but then, by declaring it aloud, you suddenly felt it drawn closer to you, fully within reach?

This is a manifestation in action. Whether you intend to address it or not, the universe is listening to you, so proclaiming your desires and self-esteem clearly can have an amazing ripple effect on your life. It can amplify your confidence, strengthen your resolve, encourage feelings of gratitude, and help you to maintain positive energy. Just be sure to project your truth without distortion, and be careful not to ask the universe for anything you aren't prepared to receive.

Use verbal or written affirmations during any self-love practice (yoga, meditation, bathing, or even while getting dressed in the morning, if you are pressed for time) to encourage self-love, drive motivation, and stay focused on your personal goals and values. Manifestation will be more focused on the future, whereas affirmations influence your current perceptions of reality. Remember that our thoughts shape our realities, so the simple act of reframing negative thoughts through the language of gratitude can change your entire outlook on life.

Journaling

There is no right or wrong way to use this practice. Regular free-writing is a fantastic way to find greater clarity of thought, as well as to self-soothe unexpressed frustrations or concerns. It may also be helpful to read over past entries from time to time, like a detective, whenever you suspect interference from a phantom source of negativity in your energy field. Journaling will help you to note healthy and risky patterns in your own behavior, as well as within the framework of your interpersonal relationships. It will also be cathartic, helping you to let go of negative feelings and leave them sealed in the past.

Chapter 10: Programming Your Subconscious Mind

As you train, the brain will create new neural networks and improve existing ones. As a result, our picture of the world will become more complete; we will no longer pass important information past us, which means that the work of our intellect will be much more productive than before.

Consider: what is more in your picture of the world—visual images, sounds, sensations? Do you perceive the world brightly and fully? Doesn't it happen that you don't notice something important, skip past the ears, or don't react to the signals that the body sends (it sometimes gives us not less important information than the one that is visible to the eyes and heard by the ears)? Based on incomplete or misunderstood information, we inevitably draw wrong conclusions and make wrong decisions. That is why you need to develop your brain map, training it for full-fledged visual, auditory, and kinesthetic perception.

Start Thinking Three Times More Efficiently!
And now, about the most important thing. Our type of perception depends on the style and quality of our thinking. We can say that visual thinking is peculiar to the visual, the audial to the auditory, kinesthetic to the kinesthetic. What does it mean?

The visual perceive any problem and task through visual images. He sees the problem. In addition, he also needs to see the decision, literally, in the form of a clear and precise picture, even if it is imaginary, even if it reflects the desired future, but he needs exactly the picture. If he does not see a picture corresponding to his solved problem, realized desire, or achieved the goal—he is unlikely to be able to get what he wants.

The audial perceives all vital tasks, mainly through hearing. Facing a problem, he wants to hear as much as possible in connection with it. In addition, how to solve the problem, he needs to hear.
Kinesthetic guided by feeling. He feels the problems and, before solving them, must feel how the problem can be solved.

Thus, not only the analysis, perception of the world, each person approaches from the point of view of his leading style of thinking—but also the solution of problems and tasks, the construction of his life, the creation of something new in it. The visual recreates his visual images in reality, the audial—what he heard and voiced, kinesthetic embodies into reality what he could feel, feel even without words and pictures.

Can you imagine how good it would be if we could both see and hear, and feel the problem and its solution? We would have learned three times more about the problem and how to solve it! Moreover, most importantly, we would get three times more opportunities to realize our desires, achieve goals; that is, we would have three times more ways to succeed!

This is precisely the purpose of this manual—to develop to the maximum extent all three types of thinking: visual, auditory, and kinesthetic.

Further Work: From Theory to Practice

At this point, we end up with the theory and proceed to practice.
- By external signs to determine who you are—visual, audial, or kinetics
- Be tested and make more accurate conclusions about the prevailing sensory channel

Carefully read all the following materials and be sure to complete all the proposed tasks. Only after that, it will be possible to proceed to the following topic—the actual training of the intellect.

Signs to help you know who you are—visual, audial, or kinesthetic

Introspection: What Do You Remember First?

Remember some meaningful or just a pleasant, memorable event from your life. What is remembered first—what you saw, what you heard, or what you felt?
Each event is stored in memory in the form of a certain set of images. These are visual images reflecting what you saw, auditory images formed from the sounds surrounding you, and kinesthetic images based on the experienced sensations. After analyzing which images prevail when you try to remember an event, you can understand which category you belong to—are you a visual, audial, or kinesthetic.

Did you immediately "see" a bright picture in your imagination? This is a sign of a visual. Poorly remember the picture, but the sounds, voices, and spoken words were well imprinted in the memory? This is a characteristic feature of the audience. Sounds and visual images are vaguely remembered but do you remember well your own sensations—heat or cold, relaxation or tone, vigor or fatigue, and also remember the smells perfectly? The chances are good that you are kinesthetic.

If it is still difficult for you to determine what type you are, take a paper and a pen and, without thinking, describe any situation in your life. Not necessarily in detail—you can restrict brief phrases. Write what comes to mind; do not think too much about the wording. Re-read, paying attention to the definitions. Do they refer to visual, auditory, or kinesthetic imagery?

Different people will describe the same situation in different ways. For example:
- Option 1. Blue sea, high mountains covered with green forest, bright pink sunset, snow-white seagulls soar in the azure sky among white clouds.
- Option 2. Loud cries of seagulls, the roar of the sea surf, the rustling of the wind in the branches, the distant echo in the mountains—nothing more breaks the silence.
- Option 3. Affectionate, warm sea waves, stones heated by the sun, clean air, which is so pleasant to breathe deeply.

Undoubtedly, you have already understood that option 1 belongs to the visual, option 2 to the audial, option 3 to kinesthetics.

Having determined which channel you have is the most used and active, select from the three topics, the one that relates to this channel, and perform all the exercises sequentially.

This is necessary to make your strengths even stronger. It would seem what is the point—because the strengths are already strong. However, the fact is that to have a strong side is one thing, but to be able to use it is completely different.

The ability of a visual, audial, or kinesthetic is akin to talent.

For talent to bear fruit, it is necessary, firstly, to learn about it, secondly, to develop it, and, thirdly, to apply it in practice.

After all, if you are, for example, a visual, then you best assimilate information that comes in a visual, visible form. Consequently, having learned to isolate visual signals in the surrounding information environment accurately and instantly analyze them, you will repeatedly increase your thinking abilities and begin to orient yourself much more effectively in all situations, quickly and more accurately understand what is happening, make the right conclusions and make the right decisions.

The same applies to audials and kinesthetics—by isolating audio signals and kinesthetic signals that are close and comprehensible to themselves, they will also begin to live and think much more efficiently. For this, you need training. Thanks to it, you will learn how to use better your natural abilities, which means to make the best and most correct decisions, to act more efficiently, to achieve success in anything, and more easily and quickly to solve the most complex problems. Moreover, all thanks to the fact that you are thinking will become perfect.

Attention is the most important factor in shaping the strength and effectiveness of your intellect. Many people do not know how to think effectively simply because they are absent-minded and inattentive. In the part of each topic devoted to attention, you will master the exercises, thanks to which you will not miss the visual, auditory, or kinesthetic signals that are important for you.

Creating visual, auditory, kinesthetic images trains the creative, creative possibilities of your mind. The only one who thinks creatively can find the best solution to any task and can generate ideas leading from success to success. "Translation" of any information into a "language" that you understand (for example, visual images—into sensations, sounds—into pictures, etc.) is a skill that will help you to catch much more signals from the surrounding reality and understand them much better to make more correct conclusions and act more effectively.

Problem-solving involves actively using your lead channel first to see it, hear or feel it most fully, and because of this, turn on the intellect to its fullest to figure out, draw conclusions, and then again see, hear, or feel the solution using your lead channel and bring it to life. Also in this part, you will learn how to get rid of unwanted memories, problems stretching from the past, to improve your mood and psychological state, to get at your disposal more strength and energy.

Achieving success will cease to be a problem when you use your leading channel at full power and, as a result, all the power of intelligence. In this part, your abilities are used both to reproduce and to create visual, auditory, or kinesthetic images. You will learn how to create your own way of success and customize your mind for its realization.

Every reader needs to go through only one of the topics 5, 6, and 7—at least for a start. After completing all the exercises in the topic on training your active type of perception, you can proceed to the other topics.

How Often to Do the Exercises?
Desirable every day. Just one exercise per day is enough. If you have time and desire, you can do 2–3 exercises a day. No longer, need not overdo it.

How Many Times to Do Each Exercise?

As much as you want, if you feel that from the first time not everything worked out, as you would like, repeat it again. You cannot immediately but after a break. You can repeat the other day and every other day. Clear rules do not exist here. It all depends on your desire.

What Time to Do the Exercises?

It is undesirable to perform most exercises immediately before bedtime—otherwise, you can fall asleep during the exercise or, conversely, the exercise will prevent sleep. As soon as you wake up, it is also better not to do it, since exercises, as a rule, require an active state of consciousness. Otherwise, there are no restrictions—work at any time of the day convenient for you.

Chapter 11: New Attitudes Regulation

Far too many people are going to come alongside in your life who have this unbeatable attitude, and when they are determined that they are going to get something, they go and get it. Every day is equally important to them because they are always doing something productive as they have an unstoppable mind. They are also mentally healthy; otherwise, maintaining this attitude wouldn't have been possible. So, if you want to become like this, here are eight things that you should do.

Develop the Freedom to Act on Instinct

The first step towards becoming genuinely unstoppable is to develop an attitude where you have complete trust in yourself. You need to be the master of the craft you are pursuing and why you shouldn't be? You are doing it all day, and you are spending hours perfecting it. This act should come to a point where you don't have to think. You will know what you are doing, and you can act based on that. That is what is known as trusting your instincts – which feeling within tells you what to do.

You will often find people telling you that they are successful today because they listened to their inner voice. You have to do precisely that. Listen to what your gut is telling you to do. You fail only when you think that you have already lost. Until then, you are still on the battlefield. Everything is in your mindset. When you feel this is the bottom of the universe, it sure will be, but if you think that you can make it till the end, you will. If you are facing difficulty in following your instincts, then you need to commit yourself fully. When you do that, you'll know that you can follow your ideas through and that you can do it.

Don't Make External Rewards Your Source of Motivation

It feels good when you have all the nice things in life but are they enough to keep you motivated? The answer might seem to be yes as for now, but it is never about prestige, money, or any other such external rewards. Are you doing what you are doing for money or for gaining more power at the workplace? When the response is yes, therefore, the degree of optimism is inadequate. Whenever your motivation is based on something like this, which is not something that interests you or is a passion to you or it is based on feeling imposed, then your motivation will not last long.

You will never have the vitality or energy to accomplish your goals until and unless you do it because you love it. According to research, people might end up reaching their goals even with suboptimal motivation, but in such cases, they cannot usually keep up with the effort in the long term. When you are pushing your limits without having any healthy dose of motivation, you will not only be lagging behind but also face mental health issues. You will start procrastinating and getting out of bed every morning to seem like a complicated task.

Never Be Satisfied but Be Grateful

You can easily ward off any unhappy feelings when you are grateful. But not being satisfied will help you push your limits and be unstoppable. When you are not satisfied, it means that it is not about the goal to you. Instead, it is about the journey and the climb to reach that goal and all those things you learn along the way. The climb will open your eyes as to how much you can push yourself.

But even if you are showing this behavior, you need to stay grateful and humble because that will keep you grounded.

Moreover, if you can hold on to this attitude, you will never get lazy or complacent. If you linger too much in your moment of success, you will become stagnant. So, it would help if you thought about the next stop – the next goal. This is how you will keep walking towards better things with an unbeatable attitude.

Live Life on Your Terms
Never let society tell you what you should do or how you should do it. It is indeed your choice, and you're meant to live it on your principles. Build the confidence and self-respect you need to do what your heart is telling you to do. If you feel that there is something about your life that you don't feel to be right, then it is time that you take matters into your own hands and change it. Sometimes people, for the most part, think the grass is always greener on the opposite side. But in reality, someone from the other side of the fence will think that the grass is greener on your side. So, in short, the grass is green on both sides, and you have to realize it.
You must also keep away from all these negative people that come into your life. Yes, they will try to point out mistakes, and they will also try to make you unhappy, but if you don't pay heed to what they say, you will not be affected by them. So, whenever you notice these negative people in your surroundings, you'll know that it is time for you to ditch them for your good.

Don't Let Off the Pressure
Indeed, some people don't perform well when they are under pressure, but in some moments, the pressure is what keeps you going. Most people in this world can function when exposed to small doses of pressure, but in the end, even they tend to relax by letting off the pressure. So, if you think you are genuinely passionate and unstoppable, you

should handle that pressure effectively without letting it hurt you. It will keep you active and alert, but only if you let it.

For this, you need to change your mindset. You cannot view pressure as something that is threatening. It would help if you saw it as a fun challenge. Whenever you see a threat, your self-confidence will be undermined, and you cannot let that happen. It can even lead to impulsive behavior. But if you try and shift your thoughts and see the pressure as a challenge, you will be doing way better. See the pressure situation as an opportunity to push your limits and grow. Also, stop worrying about the outcome. You need to put all your focus on the task that you are currently doing.

When all your concentration is on doing great in the task and not wasting time thinking about the outcome, you will only be seeing the steps in front of you, which serve as micro-goals. For example, consider a student who is writing his/her paper. If he/she concentrated entirely on coming up with stellar research, the paper would turn out to be good, but if the student wastes time thinking about what grades he/she is going to get, then all of that energy will be wasted for nothing.

Don't Compete With Others
In today's world, you will often find others acting competitive with others in their vicinity. They often end up comparing their achievements and everything else with what others have done, and this is not healthy. If you do this, you will end up staying stuck in an eternal rat race. Yes, there will always be competition, but you should not compete with others. The only person you should compete with is yourself. If you are in the habit of continuously checking what others are doing, then you need to stop it at once.
Chase your future self rather than competing with those

around you. In most cases, a person's competitive nature is often attached to cruelty, but it shouldn't have been something like that. Instead, competitiveness should be correlated with betterment and ambition. But in some cases, you will come across people who have such a giving and team-oriented attitude, and yet they are inherently competitive. What you have to do is that you have to strike a balance between being competitive and also being supportive of the same level. Only then can you funnel all your energy into doing something positive.

Always Seek to Learn New Things
If you truly want to master what you do and be the best at it, you need to keep learning. You need to enhance your skillset and find newer ways in which you can improve your skills. You will always gain power from your unparalleled preparation. Every person who has made it big in this world never pretends to know everything because they understand that there is always something new to learn. This is even truer now where technology is being upgraded with each passing minute.

Sometimes, you might feel frustrated to gain some new skill or learn something new. But no matter how challenging the task is, the happiness that you will get after completing is something that you cannot compare with anything else. Moreover, the more you learn, the more adapting you become, and the person who knows how to adapt is the person who is most valuable to any team. Your mental toughness is not defined by how well you give solutions but by the fact that how well do you adapt to varying circumstances that come your way.

Own Your Mistakes
We have already spoken about how failure is a prerequi-

site to success, and you can learn a lot from it. But in between all of it, there is another thing that people often seem to forget. You have to own up to your mistakes, too, if you want to accept the failure. You can get stuck amidst some grave long-term implications if you do not learn to own your mistakes. Whenever individuals don't own their errors, it usually leads to problems later on, and it is something like adding fuel to a spark. The problem usually keeps expanding and gradually takes a form that you cannot contain later on.

When you point fingers at others when, in reality, it is you who has made a mistake, it shows a lack of integrity and something that a leader should not do. Have you thought about what kind of an example you are setting for your team when blaming others for things of your own doing? You will not have a team if you keep behaving in such a manner. When you honestly start claiming your errors and show a proactive approach towards them, everyone will see you in a better light.

Chapter 12: Calming Worries and Anxiety

Worries and Anxiety

We all have worries in our hearts and minds. We worry about putting on too much weight, how much money we have, the snowball of bills that come into our mailbox each month, and all the other things that affect our lives. Although that is a normal thing for most people, some people struggle with depression and anxiety as a result of life's worries. Their concerns severely affect their ability to function properly and do things in everyday life. This is a stumbling block to helping people get on the road to where they want to be. We are now going to talk about how to deal with life's worries and anxiety and act appropriately.

Fight or Flight

When it comes to dealing with life's problems, different people act in their own way by facing a problem or by fleeing the scene. Many people get tempted to run away from scenarios that could get them into trouble and put them into an unfortunate situation. If you can avoid such a situation, you can also flee from the stress of that situation. However, it is not always possible to avoid such situations. Sometimes you have to face the problems of your life, as Maria said in The Sound of Music. It is, therefore, best to figure out ways that you can respond to the things that are stressing you out.

One way to combat stress is to exercise. Then you can fight the worries that are clouding your mind. Exercise is one way to get rid of stress by releasing endorphins. You can feel good after one workout, which will help improve your mood and relieve you from the burdensome cares of life. Exercise will also help you feel less nervous.

The fight-or-flight response is our body's natural instinct that we can use for our benefit. It is our coping mechanism when faced with naturally difficult situations. Our fight-or-flight response can help us to escape situations that could be dangerous to us. For example, when a fierce animal is coming toward us, we respond by running away from the place. It is important to bear in mind that it can help us or hinder us from moving forward with our lives. But the most important thing is to learn how to face our problems.

Structured Problem-Solving

Before you deal with a problem, it is crucial that you first think of the best way to respond to the situation. When you do a simulation, you will know how you should deal with a particular situation. This will help you solve the problem. If you usually worry a lot, you will find that you will feel better after confronting your problems proactively with an understanding of the issue. This way, there will be no surprises, and you will be able to handle the situation in a positive way. Solving problems is going to help you experience greater happiness. When you know how to handle all the challenges that life throws your way, you will feel better and more confident.

Limit Your Consumption of Media

Technology has a lot of benefits for us, but it can also prove to be harmful. There's no doubt that social media can be a source of stress in our lives. We compulsively check Facebook or Instagram for the latest notifications, and then we see messages that make us worry. However, if you intentionally limit your screen time and your interactions on social media, you will find that it is liberating, and you will be free of the chains that bind you to your online profile. In addition, you will experience fewer things that distract you. This will give you more productivity in your life. Try to spend a month without the distraction of social media. Get away from it for a little while and see the difference in your overall morale. You will feel much better.

Too many of us spend over four or five hours on our phones every day. We answer messages, spend time on Facebook, surf the web, watch movies, and do other things. Consuming more media is going to lead to more stress, and therefore, we should be mindful to avoid it as much as possible. Limit your screen time to only a few hours a day; you will feel better. Read a book. Go outside and enjoy the sunshine. Take a walk. Do some recreational activities that will get you out of the house and into the world? It will feel like you've made a major upgrade to your life.

Try Meditation or Aromatherapy

When you feel burdened by the weight of everyday stresses, you might feel that there is no way to get out of it. However, you should simply find a place where you can be quiet and relaxed with some soothing music that will calm your mind. Find a place where you can allow the stress to pass away. Furthermore, you can enhance this experience by including some aromatherapy. So, get some candles and scented oils that will put you in your happy place and calm your spirits. You will feel like the clouds have lifted from your mind and that the sun has come out and is shining over your heart and mind. It's a new day. Enjoy it! You deserve to be happy. Be good to yourself.

Take a Shower or Hot Bath

Another method that will help you feel loads better is if you jump into the shower or take a hot bath. You will feel that your muscles relax, and your whole body will feel a lot better. So go right ahead. Get into the water. Experience the joy of the stress being rinsed away with the water that is flowing gently against your skin. As you soak your body in the water, you can exfoliate your skin and feel the difference. You can also try aquatic therapy. Visit your local pool and allow yourself to swim the stress away. You will feel the difference, not only in your physical body but also in your mind. It is a full-body experience that you will not regret doing.

Exercise

To cope with your everyday stress, your de-stress, and one of the ways to do this must be through exercise. It is best to find an activity that works for you. There are many options that you can choose from. Aerobic activity is helpful to release endorphins, which will make you feel good and have a greater mood. Then you can feel the physical and mental health benefits.

If you don't want to do too much exercise, you can simply do a lot of walking. When you start to feel worried, go outside and take a walk. Even better, you can take a brief, intensive power walk or jog that will give you the freedom and mobility you have never experienced before.

Rest and Experience Freedom Like no Other

One of the things that we tend to neglect in our lives is getting enough rest. We power through the day and go on with our limitless supply of caffeine in our coffee and other energy drinks. We find ourselves spending more time on the computer. And often, we answer work-related inquiries well into the night while getting five or six hours of sleep. We just don't know how to take a load off and get away from work. That is especially the case with people who live in the United States who are prone to workaholism. We work more than ever before. We put on more weight than before and live an unhealthy lifestyle. One of the things that we need to learn how to do is rest and get more of it. We must rest and relax from all the cares of this life. Think about ways that you can do this.

1. Sleep Like a Baby at Night

Sleep is one of the most neglected things when life gets busy. However, we should remember that if we get more sleep, we feel healthier and happier. Getting enough rest at night is one of the ways to improve our quality of life. We can feel a lot better if we just get the right amount of shut-eye, and that usually amounts to eight to nine hours of sleep a night. I know you may be thinking, "How in the world am I going to be able to do that with my busy schedule, three kids to take care of, wife to love, etc.?"

Well, you should make sleep an important part of your wellness routine. Aside from giving you the physical benefit of feeling at your best, sleep gives us a mood boost, and we don't need to rely on as much caffeine in our system. Instead, we feel like we have more energy, and then we can go about our day with feelings of happiness. Try to get more sleep at night, and you will feel the significant change it brings to your overall health. Plus, you'll protect your body against diseases and illnesses that can easily bring you down. Sleep more for your health.

2. Go Right Ahead and Take That Nap

Napping also has proven health benefits. Even a short 20-minute nap can boost your mood and give you the needed energy to keep going through your day. Sometimes, naps can help you recover from the effects of sleep deprivation and can improve your productivity. You can try it out and see how much better you will feel. Just don't nap too much because it might mess with your sleep cycle, making it difficult for you to fall asleep at night. Be careful but enjoy it!

3. Sometimes, It's Just Doing Nothing

Sometimes, rest does not involve any kind of activity. It just involves doing nothing, whether that is hanging out on the beach, swimming in a pool, taking a walk, or sitting in a given place. You can also practice meditation. Sit quietly in a given space and simply observe your surroundings. Just looking at things and staring out into space may seem like a waste of time and energy, but the thing is, resting contributes to your productivity. And you don't need to be productive every hour of the day. Instead, you should try to find moments where you can recharge your energy. Many times, by spending time alone, especially for introverts.

4. Do Some Restful Activities, Such as Walking the Dog or Writing in Your Journal

Another thing you can do is find restful activities that don't involve too much thinking or reflection. That includes walking the dog or writing in your journal. It helps you externalize your feelings, and it makes you feel better and more energized afterward because you are not focused on the things that you must do. Instead, you choose this kind of activity. You do it because you want to, not because it's on your to-do list. It is something that will give you genuine joy, and you carry that joy with you no matter where you go.

5. Spend Time With a Few Good Friends

Depending on your personality, socializing can either be an energizing experience or a draining one. However, most people think that it can be inherently helpful to spend time with a few good friends, playing some ball, watching a movie, or even traveling together. That can be a very restful time for everyone involved. You will see how much better you feel when you can spend a good time with your close friends. The rest will be fantastic.

Case Study

David was a workaholic dad who always spent time at the office. Often, he had no idea how he could turn off his inner world. He always felt he was on-call. He had to get his kids to soccer practice, go to the office to complete a project, and get dinner from the nearest take-out center. Even then, he would lie in bed at night and worry about all the things that he had to do the next day.

He could never get rid of all the worries and rest. But then he saw a counselor who helped him to identify what things he could cut out of his life to make him feel more fulfilled and less stressed and worried about the minute cares of life. David practiced mindfulness and meditation. He started to spend more time sitting and doing nothing. In addition, he tried to implement cat naps into his day, which instantly boosted his energy and productivity. Later, he worried less and began to sleep a lot better at night. He started to turn off his notifications past 9:00 p.m. He stopped answering work-related inquiries and found himself with a better work-life balance.

In the end, everything worked out, and David felt the difference in his mind and body. David was finally able to figure out how to rest and get rid of his worry and anxiety, which plagued his mind, body, and soul. In the end, he became a much happier, more relaxed, and more productive man. It was fantastic!

Chapter 13: How to Declutter Your Environment

Principles of a Minimalist Approach
Less Is More
In his Nicomachean Ethics, Aristotle talked about how most of our relationships are based on utility and convenience and are empty of any value. However, when we hold on to one or two valuable relationships, we place importance on those relationships that contribute to our overall well-being. When you can focus on a few really good relationships, you'll enjoy your life a lot more because you'll worry less about what others think of you and think more about how you can live a happier life.

Let Go of Toxic Relationships
The second thing that you must do is get rid of every toxic relationship that is a bad influence in your life. One example of this kind of relationship is when a person sucks all the energy out of your life and plays the needy victim. Victims play the role of the victimizer, and they zap you of your needed resources. Eventually, they will take every trace of life from you if you are not careful. Victimizers can also become the center of our lives. And when that happens, you cannot do what you want to do because you have to take care of a very needy person. Instead of holding on to this toxic relationship, you should try to get rid of it as soon as possible. Surely, it will be difficult for you to relinquish your hold on this relationship because you may have invested a lot of time and energy into it, but it will be better to get rid of it sooner rather than later.

Be True to Other People
In today's world, an authentic man or woman is to be exal-

ted. Being real is something that people in society need to do to live better lives. Being a con artist and lying to others is something that is easy, manipulative, and evil; but our world is filled with such people. It harms your image, and it can also hurt your soul. One of the best things that you can do for yourself and others is to be true to yourself and other people. This way produces less stress and enables you to live a life that is going to bring you greater happiness in the end. If you want to be a true leader or manager, authenticity is increasingly important because people look up to you and trust you to do your job the right way. If you don't do that, they may look elsewhere for work. The basic principle that should underlie all of this is to never compromise on principles in your life.

Live Your Life in Relation to the Here and Now

Humans tend to look to the distant past and hold feelings of unforgiveness, or they think endlessly about the future. Both of these methods are not at all productive. We must keep our eyes focused on present circumstances, and this applies to our relationships. There is no better way to help a friend than to be for them here and now. Your friends need you now. Your wife or husband needs you now, and your kids need you now. Don't waste too much of your time surfing the web, working, or doing other things. Instead, you should prize the relationships that you have at this moment and not compromise on them for anything.

Get Rid of Unreasonable Expectations of Others

Another thing that you need to do is to release the burdensome expectations that you have of other people. This is an essential part of your friendship or love relationship. When you maintain clear and reasonable expectations for your relationship, you will experience a smoother and easier relationship with whomever. Many people have unreasonable expectations of their spouse, significant other, or friend.

This will only lead to heartbreak and friction in the relationship. Breakups and divorce can be the worst result of these expectations. Therefore, it is crucial to maintain good relationships with others while getting rid of the unreasonable expectations we may have of other people.

Connect With Your Friend or Partner Deeply
In relationships, it is crucial that you go deep rather than seeking more. When you get to know someone deeply, it will require a significant investment of time and energy. Most of our relationships will be based on a shallow level, and they will disappear when the person goes out of our life. It could be that the person moves away from us or a work situation changes. In true relationships with others, permanence should be a key marker of the relationship. Do you spend most of your time talking to your friend about sports, Netflix, or something else superficial, or do you spend more time talking about deeper and more philosophical things? It is worth finding out more about how you can spend more time on the deeper things of life, rather than dwelling on the fruitless and meaningless things that simply don't matter. Going deep will help you to have deeper connections with people.

Focus and Share Experiences
Spending time with friends, family, or other people in our lives allows us to have shared experiences that will last a lifetime. When you make the most of these times together, you can create amazing memories. Such memories will remain in your mind and heart for a long time. These memories are more important than the material stuff we acquire. They will point us to something deeper inside of us that we can share.

Intentionality
Having intentionality is an important aspect of creating good relationships. When you are intentional about your different

relationships, you can have smoother and more effective communication, which will help your relationships get off the ground in a better way. Find a purpose for spending time with your friend or partner, and you will find that the time spent will be helpful to get you in the right place. Intentionality is going to improve your friendships, love relationships, and family relationships.

Love Your Neighbor

The way to pursue a meaningful relationship with another person is through love. This is not the kind of erotic love that we are accustomed to thinking about. Instead, it is a concept of human love that applies universally. It is a love for a brother or neighbor that defines how a person can live a more meaningful life. Love should permeate your interactions with other people. It also makes things a lot prettier and less messy because what defines your relationship is what you can give to the relationship rather than what you can get from it. This makes it a less stressful kind of relationship.

Pursue Relationships With Passion

One final point is that we need to pursue our relationships with passion. We should not settle for less than excellence. Pursuing relationships requires dedication and commitment. Many people don't like to commit to things because they are afraid or too busy, but you can stand out from the crowd and commit to a relationship, whether that is with a friend or significant other, and that can be an amazing thing for your life. So, find things that you can do to spice up your life by associating yourself with wonderful people who will be beneficial to you and who can help you down the road to success in your life.

Your Home, Your Digital Life, and Your Activities

Now that we have looked at the benefits of decluttering your home, let's get creative about how to declutter your home. These simple, yet effective tips will get you started on how to declutter your home.

Determine the Department of the House You Want to Start Decluttering

This is the first and foremost step you need to undertake. You can't declutter all the areas of the house in a day. Even you do, that means you, leaving work, school, or that vital task that you were supposed to handle for the day. It can be so overwhelming if you think you can declutter your home in a day, especially if it's your first time. It can also be time-consuming, so you need to decide where you are going to start decluttering. It could be your bedroom, bathroom, kitchen, sitting room, dining, or even the garage. Start with the easiest one so that you won't get tired easily. Then, ascend to harder areas. When you have chosen an area to declutter, it's time to move to the next step on this list.

Give Yourself 5-10 Minutes Decluttering Period

Decluttering is a gradual process. A process that you ought not to rush. You can dedicate 5 or 10 minutes of your time every day to declutter your home. As you proceed, increase the time and add more tasks to your list as you go on. For example, the first day can be 5 minutes. The second can be 10, the third can be 15, and so on. Don't start decluttering with 10 minutes on your first day and spend 5 minutes the next day. It simply won't work. Before you realize it, you are finding it hard to dedicate even a minute t declutter your home. Start with the lowest possible time (5 minutes at least) and ascend accordingly.

Get a Trash Bag Ready

You would want to get rid of those items that are causing your home to be cluttered. Get a trash bag, throw them inside. Old items that you feel you don't want to get rid of, give them to charity. If you're going to store any item, get large boxes. Move them to the appropriate places and create space in your home. You will be amazed to see the number of trash bags that you have taken away.

Create a To-Do List of Items You Want to Throw in the Trash
Surely, there will be a good number of items in trash bags that you would want to get rid of. Get a paper, write out all the items that you want to get rid of. Each item that you take to the trash crosses them on your list. Also, it's important you create a to-do list of all your tasks, so that you cross each one you have accomplished. As you get rid of each item, the clutters get reduced. Creating these lists will help you keep track of tasks that you have completed and the ones that you haven't. It's easier to declutter if you have a picture of where and how to get started.

Dedicate to Remove One Item Everyday
Each day that you decide to clutter your home, try to at least get an unwanted item out of your home. Imagine doing this for a month? That's 30 items. Do this for a year, and you must have for rid of 365 items. How about you increase it to 2 items every day? In no time, you will be able to declutter your house and get those items thrown into the trash. Your home will stay completely clean and devoid of dirt.
The same thing goes for cleaning the house. Most people who do 9-5 jobs often have a hard time cleaning the entire house, and it's quite understandable. It will take your time. If you aren't able to clean your whole house, start by cleaning one part. You can just decide to clean your sitting room for that day and clean another room the following day. The most important thing is to establish a goal and stick towards it.

Take a Picture
This isn't necessary, but it's quite helpful. You can decide to take a picture of a cluttered area, like your kitchen and then,

take another picture of your kitchen. This time, a decluttered one. Observe those photos, and you will see how proud you have become that you have begun the step in decluttering your home.

Chapter 14: Panic Attacks

A panic assault can happen for apparently no explanation and has been portrayed by sufferers as the most alarming background of their life. On the off chance that you have ever encountered this you likely need to know one thing rapidly; would you be able to fix panic attacks? A great many people will involvement with at least one panic assault in their lifetime, anyway for other people, panic attacks become a piece of their regular daily existence. This everyday panic leaves them edgy to fix panic attacks so they can continue an ordinary life.

Restoring these attacks is definitely not a straightforward thing; it isn't simply a question of taking an enemy of panic pill and proceeding onward. You should survey your specific manifestations and causes with a restorative expert and after that settle on an appropriate activity plan. These attacks have been known to be misdiagnosed since other ailments can firmly imitate them. Respiratory failures, stroke, and hyperthyroidism would all be able to have comparative indications and ought to be precluded before you endeavor to fix anxiety attacks throughout your life.

There is a particular arrangement of criteria used to analyze these attacks in people and an appropriate appraisal must be finished. The criteria incorporate however isn't restricted to; rehashed attacks, at any rate, one assault pursued by a month of steady worry over having another assault, stress over going insane, or changing your conduct as a result of the attacks. Notwithstanding the above criteria, the attacks must not be related to another disorder, for example, over-the-top habitual disorder (OCD) or incited by medication misuse.

You are having a panic assault, you feel as though you are going to blackout, and your head is turning near and the air is getting thick. You are feeling alarmed, this is the subsequent panic assault in one day. Relieving panic attacks needs to turn into your main need. You are not the only one, a huge number of people experience the ill effects of anxiety and panic disorders. A panic assault can happen whenever, and there is normally a trigger that makes it happen. Panic attacks don't separate, they can happen anyplace and to anybody. Two strategies can be utilized to fix panic attacks.

Panic Attack Medical Cures
Treatment and prescription are what a specialist will prescribe to treat the disorder. Although this is a therapeutic treatment and can work, the vast majority would prefer not to take drugs that could cause undesirable symptoms. The cost is another issue with restorative fixes.

Since panic attacks don't ordinarily happen when you are in the specialist's office, it might be difficult to finish treatment if the hidden issue isn't known. The stress over the cost of restorative treatment can in itself cause a panic assault if you have no clue how to pay for the medicines and drugs.

Panic Attack Self Help Cures
Characteristic fixes are favored by many endures of anxiety and panic disorders. Characteristic cures, for example, self-improvement strategies will possibly work on the off chance that you practice the methods consistently. Since no one can tell when a panic assault will occur much of the time, you should utilize these strategies consistently.

Normal fixes incorporate changing your eating regimen and way of life. When you figure out how to eat appropriately and change your propensities, you can begin helping yourself. For certain individuals, plunking down before a fan or an open cooler entryway cools the body. At that point snacking on something that relieves you, for example, a bit of chocolate or something you appreciate can quiet you as well.

There are numerous ways for restoring panic attacks normally. You need to discover the procedure that works the best for you, however. It might require some investment, yet you will discover something that works on the off chance that you continue.

Finding the Source of a Panic Attack

If you have a panic assault, you need to attempt to recall what triggered the scene. It might have been beginning a new position or taking a ride in a vehicle that is going excessively quick. Something is triggering the panic assault regardless of whether you don't understand it. It may even be seeing your own blood or the blood of another.

Attempt to discover what is causing the panic that is triggering this scene, and you can be set up for that equivalent circumstance later on. Panic and anxiety attacks that happen obviously for reasons unknown may in any case have an explanation that you don't understand exists.

Relieving panic attacks should be possible with two distinct techniques, anyway you should pick the correct treatment for you. Simply realizing what triggers the anxiety or panic disorder is the initial step to finding a fix that works.

Chapter 15: Self-Esteem Boosters

Positive Self-Esteem
Positive self-esteem refers to a general similarity between you and others.
You are more confident about yourself, you believe in your own abilities, and you can be a happier, more successful person.
Once you know about confidence boosters and how they increase self-esteem, it's a simple job to apply them to your life.
Taking care of yourself physically and mentally increases endurance and helps you to cope with challenges every day.
Doing fun things helps you to lead a happier life.

The people you associate with and build relationships with having a drastic impact on your own worth.
Are your friends the people who keep putting you down, or are they the kind of people who praise you if you are successful?
You have to stick around people who want you to be content to have high self-esteem and be satisfied.

Protective Self-Esteem
People with protective self-esteem have positive opinions about themselves but are vulnerable and delicate to criticism. We don't know how to answer in a non-defensive way unlike people with positive self-esteem.
These types of people constantly need to be strengthened to increase their trust. They always feel the need to bring others down to feel good.

Low Self-Esteem
Low self-esteem is something many young people are dea-

ling with.

It can be a result of numerous factors, such as genetics, physical appearance, violence, abuse, and social status. Those who have low self-esteem are unable to integrate confidence boosters in their lives if their peers have positive self-esteem.

When suggestions or compliments are given, they frequently take it personally and become self-critical and nervous. We often have unsatisfactory relationships and are unable to achieve our goals.

Depression is also a low self-esteem trait. In some cases, it even gets so high that they don't know how to deal with life anymore; they tend to hurt themselves and often contemplate suicide in some cases.

Self-confidence is a part of all of us. It is a product of our experiences, our ties, our goals, and our actions.

Although living with low self-esteem can seem like a daunting, relentless struggle, it can improve.

The first move is to think about confidence boosters. The real task is to apply them. This sticks with you and influences the course of your life until you change your mindset and attitude.

Learn How to Alter Your Life With Self-Esteem

Here's a fundamental fact that I think you already know: "good self-esteem is the key to success."

Regardless of whether it is friendships, jobs, social life, or economy, you're still going to need good self-esteem. So how can we develop self-appreciation?

Let's look at it as an issue:

Simple! Easy! (I know it's not that easy, but let's do it.)

1.   Defining the Issue

Generally, self-esteem means contrasting oneself to others.

We all classify people, respect and look at some people, neglect or talk to others, deliberately or subconsciously, (horrible but real), everything is how we feel about ourselves and other people—we give ourselves a mental sign of our position in society. You think that we are worthless, everyone's better than us, and we're never going to get anywhere, you think, 'what's the point?'
It is because you have a misunderstanding about yourself, and this is the heart of the problem. Why is this a misconception? You are too self-critical because you have put poor quality on yourself when contrasting yourself with others.

2. Considering It

You are all doing the same thing, you are all being compensated in the same ways, but the shop manager has placed a $100 price tag on them and $1 on you, you're all doing the same thing so he clearly made a mistake... and imagine who is the boss responsible for putting the wrong price ticket in a store—you're the one who handles your life.

You can, therefore, correct this by increasing the price, i.e., by raising and creating your love for yourself.
Second, self-esteem is not something in your blood; you often see brothers and sisters, which have very contrasting personalities.
The good news is that it can be learned how to build up or gain self-esteem.

Interesting fact, did you know that around 60% of us have low self-esteem according to surveys?
You certainly aren't alone, though. I believe that we are not encouraged to deal with life, criticize and reverse, etc., from an early age or in school, a non-criticism seems to me—everybody succeeds mindset, but it does not teach you how to build up your self-esteem.

3.   Look at the Remedies

You need some self-analysis to get a real objective view of yourself to see how to develop self-esteem. We all have strengths and weaknesses, write them down, once we understand them, we can build on them.

What are you best at? What are you bad at? What do you like? What do you like to do? What do you want to be reasonable about? What are you doing wrong? What do you not like to do?

Next, describe what you care about. Don't think your boss or the opposite sex's congratulations are very significant, it can feel good, but it won't last.

Concentrate on bigger things. We want to know and surpass our potential and achieve things—think in this direction.

Now, everybody is different, but you must understand that you will need to improve to develop your self-esteem.

There will be nothing more if you don't. Here's a broad list, look at it, if you want to add, select the right ones, be frank, look at the strengths and weaknesses of yourself, and see how they relate.

- Self-respect. Stop beating yourself, eradicate any criticism of yourself.
- Attitude. Bad things happen; be optimistic, concentrate not on the issue but on the solution. Treat failure as a lesson and not as a reversal.
- Relationships. Mixes of positive people rather than negative ones.
- Human knowledge. Take patience, compassion, politeness, and good manners. Respect and listen to and understand other people's needs.

Take a look at your social customs. Switch embrace—don't be afraid or cynical.

Share, work, and connect. Focus on improving the abilities above, focus on them. Beset in perspective—this is the most important thing.
Visualize your career success, socially or in relationships, but have the right values.

Visualization is a powerful tool often used by sports professionals and helps you develop self-esteem.
You will consider when you learn how to build your self-esteem to be more effective in working, socially, and in relationships. It's like a downward spiral, which leads to unhappiness and hinders you from doing anything—don't give up, be determined.

The Construction of Teen Self-Esteem Starts at Birth

When does self-appreciation start? We often believe that self-esteem in our children starts when they reach two years, not realizing that it starts at birth.
It is developed from the very beginning with the influence of parental attitudes and behaviors and then continues into all development in children. First of all, they build their self-esteem by meeting their basic needs, including the need for love, comfort, and closeness.
How their parents or caregivers treat children sets the stage for the development of self-esteem.
Young babies and children who feel unloved find it harder to develop a sense of self-worth, and then take them into later childhood and adolescence.

Supportive parental behavior, including encouraging and praising accomplishments and internalizing the parent's attitudes toward success and failure, are the most critical factors in early childhood self-esteem. Stress in your home, like parents arguing a lot or having friends with whom to play and interact, can negatively impact the self-esteem and self-worth of a child at a very young age.

When kids have high self-esteem, they can deal with conflict, pressure from peers and make friends easier.
In this stage, children learn self-confidence by developing their senses of confidence, independence, and initiative with parents and siblings and then interacting with friends and relatives. Self-esteem comes from various sources for children at different developmental stages.

During our youth, our self-esteem is instilled in us. It is essential to be aware of whether the current situation at home is critical; since parents and family members blame themselves, tend to rob the child of their feelings of self-worth gradually. Self-esteem is defined as being inwardly pleasant. It is how you perceive yourself and your self-worth.

When it reflects within your child, it is what you think and feels about yourself and how well you think that you do things, it is ultimately essential, and it is on this basis that your self-esteem builds. As kids grow up and mature, and their observations move within their homes and into school and with their peers, how they determine their self-esteem becomes more critical in these areas.

Schools also have an enormous impact on self-esteem by fostering competitive attitudes and diversity and recognizing academic, sports, and arts achievements. Social acceptance by a peer group of children is essential at this stage in developing and maintaining self-esteem. The emotional and physical change in adolescence, especially in early teens, presents a child's self-esteem with new challenges.
At the time when teens undergo significant life changes, self-esteem may be very fragile; they face physical and hormonal changes. This is the moment when young people want and need a supportive family. Adjusting in your environment

is increasingly important to your self-esteem, and relationships with the opposite or sometimes same gender, in later adolescence, can become a significant source of confidence or insecurity.

Body image is a critical element of teenagers' self-esteem, and how their peers see them is of great concern.

For both boys and girls, body images are essential, and teens who like their looks and accept themselves the way they are, have high self-confidence.

Parents can encourage self-esteem by expressing their affection and support for the child and help the child to start as earlier stated in the early years; rather than imposing unreachably high standards, set realistic goals for achievement. Young people who learn to set goals in their lives have higher self-esteem than people who do not.

In this time and even before, visualization can be taught to children and adolescents.

This is an excellent tool to create and develop self-esteem for all people, and visualization videos are a great tool.

Teens could also be encouraged to watch the words they use to describe themselves; for example, if they always say they're stupid, or that they can't succeed, then, make it a habit of saying positive things and use this positive attitude to give them full self-esteem.

The use of affirmations is also an excellent way to begin with and the affirmation language, which can also be used in vision map videos.

Make sure and tell your teen that nobody is flawless in the eyes of everyone else, so they can only brace themselves for disappointment and failure by striving to become perfect.

Spend more time focusing on the things you appreciate and less on those you don't like.

Teach them to trust themselves fully, and others will also trust and believe in them.

Conclusion

Thank you for making it through to the end of Stop Overthinking; let's hope it was informative and able to provide you with all of the tools you need to achieve your goals of stopping your overthinking habits. Hopefully, you are also able to start the process of decluttering your mind as well. Additionally, let's hope you can relieve any anxiety you may have and learn how to manage your stress more effectively. This book will have also helped you to eliminate negativity in your life, control your thoughts, and stop complaining. By establishing new habits and learning some strategies for improving yourself, you may achieve new results and think the way that you want to. You will think more clearly, which will allow you to focus on achieving your goals and enjoying your life.

The next step is to integrate those habits into your life. Start by working on your focus. You may take some time to declutter, stop multi-tasking, and write down a schedule for yourself to stick to. Also, write down to-do lists for yourself to practice prioritizing and regularly do brain dumps to keep your thoughts written down. To stop worrying, you can write down all of your potential worries, take time to reflect, and talk to others. You may practice some habits to relieve your anxiety. Try taking care of your physical health, taking time to relax, and being more conscious of your mental health. Erasing negativity can be achieved by practicing good habits. You should remove negative people and places from your life, eliminate negativity from your routine, and stop yourself from complaining. You may also find more positivity in life and eliminate anything else that causes you negativity. Practicing mindfulness can also be done to help you and your mental health. You may make a conscious effort to be more mindful, or you may choose an activity to help you with your mindfulness, such as yoga or meditation.

Work on mastering your mind. Identify what you are thinking and why you are thinking that. Remember to ride your emotional waves, think more positively, and maintain control of your thoughts. To stop overthinking, you can replace your thoughts, alter your way of viewing situations, and distract yourself. You may also take time to calm down, think about the bigger picture, and remind yourself of your positive aspects. Don't let others bring you down. Take time to practice defending yourself, staying true to your beliefs, and considering if you're surrounding yourself with the right people. You may work on eliminating stress in your life by relaxing, accepting your feelings, and practicing self-care. You may also find a hobby to stick to and satisfy your senses. Work on setting goals and establishing new habits for yourself, as well as working on improving your health and having the proper mindset. These will all help you to be better.
Finally, if you found this book useful in any way, a review on Amazon is always appreciated!

Printed in Great Britain
by Amazon